T0204961

For my money, Object Lessons is the most consistently interesting nonfiction book series in America."

Megan Volpert, *PopMatters*

Besides being beautiful little hand-sized objects themselves, showcasing exceptional writing, the wonder of these books is that they exist at all . . . Uniformly excellent, engaging, thought-provoking, and informative."

Jennifer Bort Yacovissi, *Washington Independent Review of Books*

. . . edifying and entertaining . . . perfect for slipping in a pocket and pulling out when life is on hold."

Sarah Murdoch, *Toronto Star*

[W]itty, thought-provoking, and poetic . . . These little books are a page-flipper's dream."

John Timpane, *The Philadelphia Inquirer*

Though short, at roughly 25,000 words apiece, these books are anything but slight."

Marina Benjamin, *New Statesman*

"The joy of the series, of reading *Remote Control*, *Golf Ball*, *Driver's License*, *Drone*, *Silence*, *Glass*, *Refrigerator*, *Hotel*, and *Waste* . . . in quick succession, lies in encountering the various turns through which each of their authors has been put by his or her object. . . . The object predominates, sits squarely center stage, directs the action. The object decides the genre, the chronology, and the limits of the study. Accordingly, the author has to take her cue from the *thing* she chose or that chose her. The result is a wonderfully uneven series of books, each one a *thing* unto itself."

Julian Yates, *Los Angeles Review of Books*

"The Object Lessons series has a beautifully simple premise. Each book or essay centers on a specific object. This can be mundane or unexpected, humorous or politically timely. Whatever the subject, these descriptions reveal the rich worlds hidden under the surface of things."

Christine Ro, *Book Riot*

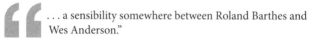

". . . a sensibility somewhere between Roland Barthes and Wes Anderson."

Simon Reynolds, author of *Retromania: Pop Culture's Addiction to Its Own Past*

OBJECT LESSONS

A book series about the hidden lives of ordinary things.

Series Editors:

Ian Bogost and Christopher Schaberg

Advisory Board:

In association with

Georgia Tech | Center for Media Studies

BOOKS IN THE SERIES

cell tower

STEVEN E. JONES

BLOOMSBURY ACADEMIC
NEW YORK • LONDON • OXFORD • NEW DELHI • SYDNEY

BLOOMSBURY ACADEMIC
Bloomsbury Publishing Inc
1385 Broadway, New York, NY 10018, USA
50 Bedford Square, London, WC1B 3DP, UK

BLOOMSBURY, BLOOMSBURY ACADEMIC and the Diana logo are
trademarks of Bloomsbury Publishing Plc

First published in the United States of America 2020

A catalogue record for this book is available from the British Library.

A catalog record for this book is available from the Library of Congress.

ISBN: PB: 978-1-5013-4881-5
ePDF: 978-1-5013-4879-2
eBook: 978-1-5013-4880-8

Series: Object Lessons

Typeset by Deanta Global Publishing Services, Chennai, India
Printed and bound in the United States of America

To find out more about our authors and books visit www.bloomsbury.com
and sign up for our newsletters.

CONTENTS

1 CELLSPOTTING

This is not a book about the cellphone, that shiny, flat computer with a radio in it that you probably have with you right now. This is a book about what makes the cellphone mobile, about the large object that connects the phone to the network—the cell tower. Communication towers of one kind or another have been around for centuries, tall platforms from which to signal using flags, lanterns, bells, or voices. But the cell tower (in the UK it's called a mobile mast or a telephone mast) is a descendant of early modern towers, and it inherited some of modernism's ambitions in its steel bones.

Nikola Tesla's Wardenclyffe Tower is a good example of those modernist ambitions. It was 187 feet tall, built on New York's Long Island in 1901 and demolished in 1917, and was meant to transmit both telegraph signals and electrical power wirelessly, using the Earth itself as the conductive medium. Or, take the Eiffel Tower in Paris (1889), which Walter Benjamin called a "monument" to the "heroic age of technology."[1] Maybe you've visited it. It's a famous architectural structure with an aesthetic aura, but the whole point originally was its iron-lattice engineering.

It stands 1,024 feet tall, with 2,500,000 rivets and 18,038 iron components—tallies like these have always been part of appreciating the iconic Tower.[2] Scheduled for demolition after twenty years, it was kept standing in part because Eiffel promoted its usefulness as a giant wireless antenna.[3] You've probably seen the animated RKO Radio Pictures logo at the beginning of old movies, a giant latticework steel tower straddling the globe and beaming out radio waves and bolts of electricity. Broadcast or telecommunications towers like these went up everywhere during the twentieth century and into the twenty-first century, from London's BT Tower, to Toronto's CN Tower, to the red-and-white Tokyo Tower (which is also an emoji), to the Skytree, also in Tokyo, and many more around the world. Tapered towers and techno-spires like these show up in the cartoon skylines of *The Jetsons*, *Futurama*, and Disney World's Tomorrowland because they once signified "The Future" (which evidently will involve lots of radio transmissions).

That future isn't what it used to be. We still depend on radio waves, on harnessing a portion of the electromagnetic spectrum, but the bulk of today's communications infrastructure has been shrunk into skinny glass fibers, running underground and underwater, often along paths originally laid for telegraph cables. Above ground, though, it's all about utilitarian steel, antennas bolted on in various configurations. Today's cell towers descend from the earlier communications towers—latticework types like the Eiffel Tower, and monopoles like the needle-shaped BT Tower—

but cell towers are actually a very different kind of object, so mundane we barely notice them. The carriers prefer it that way ("Security Through Obscurity" is a common motto). Most of us prefer it that way, too. We're too busy looking down at the little screens in our hands to notice.

Today's telecommunications networks combine wireless and wired connections. The cell tower is a kind of steel portal between the two. That wireless jump—to and from our phones—is the shortest link in the chain of connectivity, but it's the most important link to most of us, the link that makes the cellular network cellular. That network is laid out in an imagined grid of six-sided cells, like a beehive, a quilt, or a patio made of hex-block pavers. As a shape, the hexagon tessellates well, as mathematicians say, like a tile or a paver that can be laid efficiently, covering a lot of area without leaving too many gaps. Where I live, sidewalks and patios are often paved with hex blocks for this reason. The goal of the cellular telephone system is "a kind of spatial multiplexing,"[4] a way of allowing multiple signals to share a portion of the electromagnetic spectrum. In the cellular grid, a tower can be placed at the juncture of any three hexes where their edges touch, beaming its radio waves in three directions (three sectors of 120 degrees each). This is a geometry of optimization: a way to approach the ideal of ubiquitous coverage and to provide a seamless "handoff" from tower to tower as you move from place to place. In real life, though, things happen to block the connection. You may lose indicator bars on your phone, maybe drop the call.

"'You there?" you say. "I lost you." But what you've really lost is the wireless connection to an unseen cell tower, of which you suddenly become aware in its moment of failure, like a missing tooth.

Someone I know in rural Appalachia can stand in her kitchen, look out through the screen door, and point across adjacent fields to "her" tower, silhouetted up on a mountain ridge, a tapered latticework structure with a triangular rack around the top like an eighteenth-century tricorn hat, mounted with three sets of oblong white antenna panels. Cell sites in that area are so sparse she's probably right. She likely does know where her connection comes from, at least when she's in the house and yard. If she drives to the Walmart thirty miles away, she'll probably drop the signal more than once—either because she gets out of range of that tower and isn't in range of another, or because the rock-faced mountains interfere, creating radio shadows where the signal just can't reach.

I, on the other hand, drive past thirty cell towers on my forty-mile commute. That's thirty actual towers, not counting various antenna arrays mounted on rooftops or around the perimeter of water-tower tanks (I see those, too). This is in Florida, which is close to sea level everywhere, and I travel mostly on an elevated highway, so I can see pretty far—to the horizon in many places. Tall objects really stand out. In the metropolitan area of Tampa Bay, with very little public transportation, unlike cities I've lived in before, I have to make this drive several times a week, and I always feel guilty about it. One day, sitting in traffic on the bridge (plotting the purchase of an electric vehicle), I looked up and noticed all the cell towers. It dawned on me: all this infrastructure—bridge, highway, towers—none of it is *beneath* my everyday life (as the prefix *infra* might imply). It *is* my everyday life. I'm inside *it*.

Thirty is a lot of towers. Depending on where you live, you may have that many cell towers near you, too, maybe more. But do you ever really notice them? Mostly, we don't. Or rather, we prefer to unsee them, to look right through them and immediately forget we ever saw them. The cell tower is a giant piece of infrastructure we depend on every day, but we're so invested in the idea that the cellphone experience should be seamless, invisible, ethereal, and ubiquitous, we screen it out. We just don't see it looming there. We unsee it.

I began this book because I started noticing cell towers. Eventually I made a kind of game of it, developing a habit I jokingly called cellspotting.[5] Like a trainspotter—a nerdy railway hobbyist (especially in the UK) who treats transportation infrastructure the way bird-watchers treat rare species in the wild, recording the models and individual serial numbers of locomotives they see on platforms or passing by on the tracks—I look out for cell towers anywhere I travel. It all started with those thirty towers, on that fifty-minute drive from a small barrier island on the Gulf of Mexico to the urban campus where I teach, traveling over the causeway and a three-mile bridge across the sparkling waters of Tampa Bay.

On the bridge, I often see brown pelicans flying along beside the car at eye level, then disappearing as they dive for fish. Sometimes an osprey sits on a light pole to eat a fish it caught down between the concrete pilings.

One of my favorite towers stands on a narrow bar of mangroves at the edge of the land on the west side of the bay (Figure 1). Because it's so close to the road, I can see the whole

FIGURE 1 Monopole tower near the Howard Frankland Bridge, Tampa Bay, St. Petersburg, Florida. Author's photograph.

cell site, from the top of the slightly faceted monopole, to its multiple tiers of triangular panel-antenna arrays, to open portholes lower down where cables emerge and connect to the BTS (base transceiver station) equipment, including transmitters and receivers, generators, and batteries in metal containers at the base, all of it sitting on raised metal platforms to avoid the inevitable salty floodwaters, the whole site surrounded by a chain-link fence with a number-pad lock. Dense trees form a backdrop to the site. Once on the bridge, I can see several more towers. As I said, because it's so flat here, you can see all kinds of faraway tall objects; cell towers are just one kind. In fact, they resemble those tall, spindly palm trees that stick up everywhere here. The fronds at the top of a sabal palm (the Florida state tree) look very much like the array of antennas around the top of a monopole cell tower, a resemblance that (who knows?) may have inspired one of the common stealth-tower disguises. I've learned to spot different styles of towers and antennas besides those slim, tubular monopoles: triangular cross-section, tapered, freestanding steel latticework towers (the ones that look like little Eiffel Towers); very tall, straight-sided and guy-wired latticework towers, sometimes painted in alternating red and white bands, with cellular equipment bolted on about halfway up; arrays of oblong directional antennas (each panel of which I know has a column of small metal antennas behind it), arranged in threes or fours around a triangular rack, with multiple racks sometimes stacked in layers in what the industry calls colocation (co-location), the combination of more than one carrier on the same tower; white microwave drums, parabolically curved beneath flat or bulging covers, stuck on the sides of towers like mushrooms on a tree trunk, and requiring clear line-of-sight connections between them; multidirectional whip antennas sometimes protruding from the tops of towers, used to pinpoint the strength and location of phones; similar looking lightning rods; fat coaxial cable bundles running down to the ground like tropical vines, where they connect to the sheds and boxes enclosed behind a locked fence with ominous warning signs in the "ground space" at the foot of the tower. Once I began to notice cell towers, I started to see them everywhere, even if I only caught a glimpse as I zoomed by at 70 mph. I had been surrounded all along.

Earlier, I said that most of us prefer to unsee cell towers. I'm borrowing the term from the science-fiction novel by China Miéville, *The City & the City* (2009). In the story, two imaginary European city-states occupy the same geographic space while maintaining their two separate cultures—not unlike the real-world examples of Jerusalem, Berlin, or Beirut—as if they existed in parallel universes or adjacent dimensions. If you're a citizen of one of the cities, then the other city must remain outside your conscious vision. Residents are raised from early infancy to inhabit their own civic space without acknowledging the overlapping other space, taught to observe invisible but inviolable borders, to see only one of the two realities. A kind of cultural taboo compels you to unsee residents from the other city as they pass on the same street, to unsee the buildings, parks, and signs of the other city that you're are not "in," even though you're physically standing in the same geographic space. You have to practice a kind of willed blindness. (In the TV adaptation, this is represented visually by blurring half the streetscape, or the building, or the person that a character is supposed to be unseeing in a given scene.) If a momentary lapse or "breach" occurs and you happen to catch a glimpse of the other city's infrastructure or inhabitants, then you must instantly unsee or "unnotice" them, erase them from consciousness. Forbidden objects are said to be "unvisible"—not inherently *in*visible but capable of being unseen.

This fictional analogy may seem a little dramatic, but I think it's a useful metaphor for what we do every day when it comes to cellular infrastructure: we unsee it, as if in obedience to some internalized taboo. We avert our eyes or look right through it toward the horizon and continue to talk about cellphone connections as if they happened through invisible wireless magic. But the towers intrude on our awareness from time to time, stubbornly material manifestations of the system sticking right up into the air, in our face. They force us to notice them when the signal drops on our phones (I must be out of range of a tower, you think), their presence felt through their absence, like the "girdered towers" from one city in Miéville's novel, the shadow of which "would loom over" a church in the parallel city—that is, it would "if they were there." Sometimes you realize with a shudder that your location is being tracked, that Google knows where you are because your phone just pinged that tower you think you glimpsed out of the corner of your eye.[6] Sometimes a 200-foot tower shows up in your own backyard, as it were, near your kid's school, say, or in sight of your local park, commanding attention, provoking inchoate fears about potential health effects, even though you may be aware that scientific research has shown no link between the non-ionizing radiation of cell towers and damage to human health.[7] Or an intrusive tower may just strike you as aesthetically ugly or ridiculous in its failed attempt at camouflage (no one could mistake that hideous thing for a real tree!). But even when you're unaware of them, nearby cell towers are aware of you (thanks to your ever-present phone). That's just how they work. In another scene in *The City & the City,* the streets are crowded with people from the other, overlapping city, and the narrator has to keep unseeing the passersby as he hurries along in the midst of them. "I unsaw them," he says, "but it took time to pick past them all."

The cell tower is a gigantic object that remains effectively invisible most of the time, at the periphery of our vision but at the center of our everyday lives. It is linked not only to the cellular network but to structures of political power, money, social relations, and quotidian activities that shape our lived experience.[8] While writing this book I've tried *not* to pick my way past a wide variety of cell towers out in the world, tried instead to really see them and to understand them in their own right, in their local contexts. They were often weirder than I expected—more idiosyncratic and more interesting—

and this wasn't limited to examples camouflaged as pine trees, hidden in church steeples, or attached to a roadside buffalo sculpture. They embodied in various forms the stubborn materialities that support our shiny idea of cellular telephony. The cell tower remains an object worth paying attention to, even in this era of supposedly imminent 5G networks, small cells, better concealed antennas mounted on buildings and street furniture—among which tall cell towers will likely remain for some time—not to mention the possibility of cell towers in space. Learning to really see the cell tower can help us to better understand our insatiable desire for invisible, ethereal, and ubiquitous connectivity—however much steel, concrete, and cable it takes to sustain that desire.

2 INVISIBLE WAVES

Cell towers are part of the history of radio, and radio is all about invisible electromagnetic waves. The cell tower is a piece of 200-foot infrastructure, anything but invisible. But it connects to your phone via radio waves, propagated over an unseen portion of the electromagnetic spectrum. That spectrum itself is a hard thing to get a handle on, a challenge to our ideas of what's real and what's not. The large thing that cell towers help to make up—cellular telephony—is also hard to grasp, since it operates at a scale beyond everyday experience. All of these are perhaps reasons we tend to think of the network as invisible, despite its material infrastructure of concrete, steel, batteries, generators, and cables—but also human workers, money, corporations, and governments.[1] Besides, as humans, we're self-centered. The network is linked to *us* via those invisible waves, so that's what matters most to us.

Our fascination with invisible communications predates cell towers, going back at least to the era when radio was new and "wireless" was a synonym for it (especially in British English). We're not that far from the spooky discovery that encoded signals and ghostly sounds could emerge from the unseen realm having traveled over vast distances. Radio waves challenge commonsense notions about matter and energy, about what counts as real, because we can't see them or touch them, and many of us can't fully grasp the physics by which they operate. But since the late nineteenth century, we've increasingly been made aware that we live in what Anthony Dunne has called hertzian space—after Heinrich Hertz, who first demonstrated the existence of radio waves in the 1880s and for whom a unit of radio frequency is named—"a complex soup of electromagnetic radiation" we move through every day.[2] Hertzian space makes possible Wi-Fi connected laptops, surveillance doorbells, remote controls, Bluetooth beacons in stores, wireless earbuds, smart speakers, smart watches, your car's phone-linked audio and navigation system or key-fob remote, garage door openers, radio-frequency identification (RFID) tags on consumer goods, and near-field communication (NFC) chips embedded in toys or transit cards, and, yes, your cellular telephone service. We think of each of these applications as a discrete "signal" we can invoke as needed, like when we pair a speaker with our phone, but they're really more like different ways of tapping into the circumambient energy of the invisible spectrum that we inhabit—that we live inside all the time.

I have an app, Architecture of Radio, which renders hertzian space visible (and audible), representing the radio signals around me as I aim my phone in various directions, like astronomy apps that show the constellations when you point your phone at the night sky. In fact, like those astronomy apps, the Architecture of Radio shows the location of satellites in orbit. It produces visualizations, with dotted white lines in curves marked by little cell tower and satellite icons, set against a deep blue background. (It also makes electronic sounds: the hums and beeps intensify as the signals do.) But it doesn't directly sense either satellites or radio waves. The app uses my GPS location, combined with open data about known Wi-Fi routers, cell towers, and satellites, to map what I *should* find around me, creating visual representations of *potential* signals.[3] There will always be gaps between the actual radio frequency signals in a city park, say, and what the data says about signals at that location, a reminder of the uncertainties we always experience inside hertzian space. We're walking around immersed in fluctuating energies we can't see or hear but can register, though usually only approximately, through our devices.

The spooky feeling of being immersed in this way is nothing new. It goes back to the early twentieth century, when radio first emerged. You can see it reflected in the architecture of that era, as media historian Shannon Mattern has shown, for example in the RCA compound of Rockefeller Center in New York.[4] Its art-deco motifs include gilded bands of abstract waves emanating from the proscenium arch above the stage at Radio City Music Hall.[5] Stone-and-steel buildings can block transmissions in the city, but the tallest buildings of the era were convenient antenna supports. Every skyscraper had a prominent radio mast on top (it's what King Kong holds on to atop the Empire State building), a sign of modernity as much as a practical utility.[6]

Those art-deco skyscrapers were preceded by monuments like the ones I mentioned in Chapter 1: the Eiffel Tower, for example, erected for the 1889 World's Fair and scheduled to stand for only twenty years, until a radio antenna was added in 1903, effectively prolonging its life. Today the Eiffel Tower is a symbol of French national identity and tourism and has an aesthetic aura—its design is famous—but radio and TV broadcasts still emanate from it, just as radio-telegraph signals once did. The tower's design, its "latticed geometry," as Mattern calls it,[7] finds a visual echo in today's cell towers. Another historical predecessor can be seen in the cartoon tower in that RKO Radio Picture movie logo I also mentioned in Chapter 1, straddling the spinning globe and beep-beeping out Morse code (for "this is an RKO picture") while emitting bolts of electricity and radio waves in concentric circles.[8] It looks old-fashioned, now, but the logo's steel tower isn't really that different from today's latticework cell towers. With minor modifications, the logo might appear in an advertisement for a cellular telecommunications company touting its worldwide coverage. Except, today, instead of a single giant tower looming over the Earth, there would no doubt be a multitude of towers, a glowing constellation of cell sites clustered like pins on an interactive map. No one would be impressed by a single cell tower, even one as colossal as in the logo. What we want now is to be assured that there are lots of towers everywhere (more every day), there when we need one, but always already receding into the background of our attention as we check our phones.

In Shoreham, Long Island, you can visit the site of maybe the strangest radio tower in American history, Nikola Tesla's unfinished Wardenclyffe Tower, built in 1901 and dynamited in 1917 (Figure 2). A narrow stone border in a geometric pattern on the ground still marks the base where it once rose 187 feet into the air, wood latticework topped with a massive

FIGURE 2 Nikola Tesla's Wardenclyffe Tower in Shoreham, Long Island, New York. Image courtesy Iwona Rudinska, The Tesla Collection, http://teslacollection.com/images.

mushroom-cap cupola. Tesla intended for it to transmit telegraph messages wirelessly over vast distances, including across the Atlantic, and also—more radically—to transmit electrical power wirelessly, apparently using the Earth itself as a conductive medium.[9] The plan was never executed and the tower came down, but it represents an outer limit of radio-age ambitions. A science center is currently planned at the Wardenclyffe location, with the support of a million-dollar donation from Elon Musk, whose own electric cars are of course named after Tesla and whose SpaceX rockets exceed even Tesla's planetary-scale ambitions.

Tesla's rival Guglielmo Marconi performed similar experiments, including on December 12, 1901, when he transmitted telegraph messages across the Atlantic between England and Canada. The first transmitter station at Poldhu, Cornwall, on the southwest tip of England, was a series of poles arranged in a circle, a kind of weird radio Stonehenge.[10] This was destroyed by a storm and Marconi replaced it with a big antenna made of 54 wires hanging from a cable stretched between tall poles. The following year, he built an improbable gigantic wire antenna in the shape of a 200-foot upside-down pyramid suspended point-down above a small building. The whole thing was supported by four 200-foot steel-lattice towers, arranged like colossal table legs around the building. In retrospect these look a lot like modern cell towers.

Some of the sublime mystery surrounding Marconi's and Tesla's experiments clung to home radio receivers and broadcast towers when radio became commercially available in the early twentieth century. That sublimity was sometimes associated with the emergent telephone system at the time, as well, with its scribbled masses of black wires strung overhead.[11] But it was monumental telecommunication towers that continued through the twentieth century to represent the infinite possibilities of exploiting the invisible powers of the electromagnetic spectrum. Broadcast or telecom towers of this kind still stand in many cities around the world. A well-known example is London's concrete and steel BT (British Telecom) Tower (1966), a narrow spire marking the city's skyline, over 600-feet high with its antennas, signifying a space-age futurism that goes back to the radio age.

On a recent summer visit to Mexico City I noticed a lot of cell towers amid the city's glass skyscrapers, older stone buildings, ancient pyramids, and iconic obelisks, all standing, as fate allowed, in the wake of recent powerful earthquakes. On my ride in from the airport through a neighborhood with mostly two- or three-story buildings, I saw plenty of antenna arrays on rooftops, those familiar oblong panels in threes or fours, and some microwave drums on short poles. But there were also a few full-sized steel-mesh towers right there in the middle of the capital, standing on a vacant half-lot or on a low rooftop, the sort of thing US zoning wouldn't usually allow. From the highway coming in I had seen a cluster of towers—FM masts and cell towers—on a distant mountain, silhouetted against thunderclouds. It was the rainy season and an afternoon shower started before I got to my hotel.

As I passed the covered market in the San Juan district, I caught a glimpse of a strange gray concrete structure rising above the neighborhood. Its façade was cement lattice in a curved cone shape, with layers of conning platforms, a bunch of microwave-drum antennas clustered around the upper tier, and an antenna mast on top. It looked like a misshapen ear of corn with a fungus on it, or a Mesoamerican-modern version of London's BT Tower, or a brutalist air traffic control tower out on the tarmac of a mid-century airport. Then it was gone, occluded by taller buildings and the rain. Later I looked it up: it was the 367-foot Torre de Comunicaciones (Communications Tower), opened in 1973 as the headquarters of the major Mexican telecom, Telmex (Figure 3).

The next morning it wasn't raining, so I walked over to see the tower from up close. A large sign above the gate read TELEFONOS DE MEXICO. The building's concrete was cracked and some of its windows were patched with sheets of plywood. Behind the fence, two men dragged a heavy cable across the plaza. I watched from behind the locked gate, then took a walk around the block. Crossing the street to a park, I spotted another tall building about a mile to the north that looked a lot like the Empire State building in New York, a classic skyscraper with a tall antenna mast. It was the famous Torre Latinoamericana. I decided to walk to it, and the street I chose was full of wholesale and retail small electronics shops, maybe as an indirect result of the Telmex tower's being nearby. One stall I passed was selling different gauges of wire and cable.

FIGURE 3 Telmex Torre de Comunicaciones in Mexico City. Author's photograph.

Once at the tall building I rode the elevator up to an outdoor observation deck with stunning 360-degree views of Mexico City. It was a rare clear day and I could see all the way to the mountains, where I spotted that cluster of towers I had seen earlier from the taxi. About a mile to the east I could see the Templo Mayor excavation site of Mesoamerican pyramids in the city center. To the south, sure enough, I saw the tapering concrete-lattice cone of the San Juan Communications Tower that I had just left. From up there it looked small, but it still loomed over its own neighborhood near the market. Back inside, I saw a cartoon map on the wall showing the Communications Tower as one of the landmarks tourists can look for from the observation deck. According to the elevator directory, several floors of the Torre Latinoamericana were occupied by Telmex.

One website about the Communications Tower, or Torre de Comunicaciones, describes its eclectic architecture as invoking "ancient Egypt, Teotihuacán, Palenque and Uxmal."[12] The architect, Hector Mestre, blended indigenous and other ancient motifs in the design. The tower's prominent clusters of drum-shaped microwave antennas became part of its semiotics, explicit signs of its role as a beacon of "the future" beamed from the capital to the nation as a whole. In 1978 the 100th anniversary of the introduction of telephony to Mexico was commemorated at the Tower, with a ceremony that included burying a time capsule, to be opened in 2078, whether or not the tower's still standing by then. That's a serious question: a 1985 earthquake shook the site hard, partly separating the tower from the buildings at its base and interrupting the phone service. And there have been numerous earthquakes since.

Radio waves are invisible, but radio antennas are mundane physical objects, even sometimes clunky ones, that serve as gateways between those invisible waves and equally invisible electrical currents, which can be sent through fiberoptic or copper cables and transduced as sounds or images, on the one hand, or, further transduced, relayed through the air via microwaves—using another portion of the electromagnetic spectrum—back to the network at large. Historic towers like the Communications Tower in Mexico City can seem weird, now, as if they are newly discovered artifacts of an earlier civilization, in part because they are so flamboyantly semiotic, flaunting the now-obscure signs of their function like the sigils of an ancient religion. They were usually designed that way for corporate clients, aimed at maximum cultural impact to tout the power of radio communications. Their function was also practical: in one sense, towers like these were just big, building-sized antennas. They lifted transceivers high and housed the technology for connecting them to the network. But the stylized towers also revealed some of the cultural contexts of radio and telephone telecommunications, including the idea of conquering the invisible forces of the electromagnetic spectrum—never mind that companies had to apply, bid, win, and pay in order to use their delimited slice of that spectrum.[13] Such towers were signs of economic authority, as well—signs of the companies' control over the infrastructure on which people increasingly depended as the century went on.

Today's cellular system disperses much of that symbolic and economic authority out into less obvious channels. Companies compete over the ever-increasing number of towers they have on the map. But each cell tower still retains a whiff of the symbolic power once associated with early radio and telecom towers, and each cell tower stands as a reminder of the scaffolding needed to support the illusion of totally wireless communications. The key piece of that scaffolding is the antenna. The symbol for antenna in an engineer's diagram is a vertical line with an inverted triangle at the top (like Marconi's upside-down pyramid), the triangle sometimes bisected by the line. It looks like a child's drawing of a monopole cell tower. The essential function of the cell tower is to raise up antennas. But the scaffolding represented by the cell tower only stands as a result of corporate economic power and government authorization, and the use of the spectrum always has a cultural resonance.

About 300 miles southeast of the Torre Latinoamericana skyscraper in the heart of Mexico City, in the mountain state of Oaxaca, some recent experiments have looked at alternative ways to put up cell towers. The non-profit organization Rhizomatica promotes do-it-yourself community-owned cellular networks for rural portions of the country that have no coverage.[14] Their plan is to use open-source software and base-station hardware combined with welded-together scrap-metal antenna masts (even in some cases bamboo poles) only 10–12 feet tall—a size that a couple of volunteers can mount by hand on a tall rooftop or high hill in their village. These ad hoc cell towers, attached to home appliance-sized base stations, which in turn are just plugged into wall sockets, provide small-scale infrastructure for local co-ops, organized like community-owned radio stations.

This homemade tower movement arose against the backdrop of national conflict. Telmex, the company that built the Torre de Comunicaciones, is effectively a monopoly, owned by the billionaire Carlos Slim Helú, at one time the richest person in the world. Rhizomatica is David to Telmex's Goliath, taking on the quasi-monopoly and arguing that telecommunications should be a right, not a commodity. They want to reimagine the electromagnetic spectrum itself as a commons, offering shared access to communications.[15] In July 2016, the small Indigenous Communities Telecommunications company in central Mexico (TIC), was formed, the first fully licensed co-op managing a community-owned and community-operated cellular network.[16] That is, they set up a bunch of ad hoc rooftop antennas and plugged in some open-source base stations, creating a basic 2G Global Systems for Mobile Communications (GSM) network, supported with small monthly subscriptions and managed by a local board. But in such remote locations, where there was no coverage at all before, this made a difference.

In the developed world, the near-ubiquity of cellphones has led to an increased role for big telecoms in people's everyday lives, as writer and urbanist Adam Greenfield has argued.[17] Mundane activities like finding your way around, checking the weather, listening to music, making a phone call, playing a game, all depend on the intervention of hidden forces, starting with the energies of the electromagnetic spectrum, but including governments and corporations that manage access to the spectrum.[18] When we lose our connection for a moment, while trying to navigate with a GPS map, for example, we have to face what we usually just ignore: that doing everyday things now "depends on a vast and elaborate infrastructure that is ordinarily invisible to us."[19] This infrastructure is both "intangible and too vast to really wrap our heads around," which places it "on the other side of the emotional horizon" from us.[20] We know it exists but it doesn't feel real. In this context cell towers look like the return of the repressed infrastructure—looming reminders of the system we mostly try to unsee. Experiments like Rhizomatica's aren't likely to make a significant dent in the global economy of corporate telecommunications. But they serve to focus attention on our dependence on that infrastructure, which consists not just of concrete and steel, antennas, towers, base stations, computerized switches, and cables, but lucrative segments of the invisible and yet still material electromagnetic spectrum.

The Torre de Comunicaciones in Mexico City and similar radio and telecommunication skyscrapers around the world predate cell towers. They are the cell tower's weird ancestors from the radio age. Especially when they get repurposed *as* cell towers, as they frequently do, they remind us how much we still (more than ever) rely on ambient radio waves. Flamboyant urban skyscrapers were mostly displaced over the last century by a more distributed utilitarian system for radio communications, which in cities leveraged the increased number of tall buildings on which to mount antenna racks. But cell towers aren't entirely demystified in our own time, as we'll see in the next chapter, and their mystification is not entirely about the supernatural: sometimes it's a symptom of real economic and political worries about tracking, surveillance, and corporate control in general. These, too, are invisible forces that affect us. More than ever, we live in hertzian space, the possibility space that fascinated Tesla and Marconi and the early listeners to radio signals. Signs of our immersion are everywhere. But most of us prefer to keep our eyes down on the shiny devices in our hands, which have taken over as the paradoxically magical and yet mundane gateways through which mysterious wireless energies flow— allowing me to call a Lyft in Mexico City, for example, and (I hope) helping the driver locate me on her version of the app. But those devices, hers and mine, are in the end just little radios combined with computers. And they need to find a tall tower nearby in order to connect to the vast, unseen network, which we imagine as being out there somewhere, when in fact it's here all around us. We're soaking in it.

3 CAMOUFLAGE

When I told people I was writing this book, the most common response was for them to blurt out how much they hated those cell towers disguised as trees. The cell tower is a big and obtrusive object. Turning it into an ersatz tree doesn't make it any less so. So why do companies do it? And why does the attempt bother us so much?

Maybe it has something to do with our feelings about nature. People seem to be less offended by a cell site in a church steeple than by one in a fake saguaro cactus. A cell antenna on a street light rarely provokes an intense reaction—at least it didn't until recently, when 5G small-cell antennas, on light poles or their own poles, began to colonize quiet suburban neighborhoods, stoking fears and leading to protests.[1] The most intense revulsion seems to come in response to near-miss, and therefore uncanny, nature, the Frankensteinian sense that a fundamental taboo has been violated. "Only God can make a tree," as the poem says.[2] Would we be happier if the camouflage were perfect and we were surrounded by expertly disguised towers? Novelist William Gibson has a character traveling in southern California remark on "those creepy fake trees you saw from highways here, the cellular towers disguised with grotesque faux foliage, Cubist fronds, Art Deco conifers, a thin forest supporting an invisible grid . . . The net of telephony . . ."[3] Creepy, fake, grotesque—these disguises aren't just unnatural, they're bad art. And they make people mad.

Maybe that anger is also a moral response to feeling like the victim of an attempted scam. We're offended by the effort to deceive, to make the tower invisible—but also, paradoxically, by the failure of deception (do we look that stupid?). We expect cell towers to recede politely into the background, to remain as invisible as we believe the whole grid of wireless telephony is. Sincere functionalism is all we ask. No wonder we're irritated when we get insincere fake foliage, like the wire branches of a cheap artificial Christmas tree. Making a cell tower look like a pine tree costs more, and it almost never fully succeeds (assuming the goal is a perfect imitation of nature), so, again, why do cellular companies put up camouflaged towers?

Sometimes it's just an act of minimal compliance, like those patches of bright green binding ingredient that hold together clumps of fresh grass seed on suburban lawns. Nobody thinks they really look like grass, but at least they gesture toward fitting in, performing a kind of due diligence. Likewise, fake cellular trees are just trying to "soften the severity of the steel tower with botanical plastics."[4] Most cell tower camouflage is created in the spirit of military camouflage rather than mimetic imitation. It aims only to make the tower blend in, not to achieve true invisibility, but to help us suspend disbelief, to deflect our glance, and aid us in our unseeing.

Camouflage is the art of hiding something in plain sight (nothing to see here), and it has traditionally imitated nature to that end. Some animals have evolved to literally imitate other things—insects that look like sticks or leaves, for example—but many have evolved patterned or colored skins, coats, or feathers that allow them to blend in just enough with their environments, to hide by evading the gaze of predators, not by making the predators think they actually are another thing. Military camouflage mostly works the same way. It applies artificial patterns and colors of vaguely natural but abstract vegetation, sand, or rocks, just enough color and form to fool or confuse the sights of a sniper or the cameras of a drone.[5] Stealth cell towers apply both mimesis and misdirection: sometimes they imitate real things (trees, cacti, flagpoles, crosses) and sometimes they deflect the gaze by blending in just enough. In most cases, they do a little of both. What people take as an insulting failed attempt at mimetic deception, an attempt to pass as a tree, is often just an effort to somewhat better fade into the forest. One company that specializes in camouflaged cell towers sums up the limits of this strategy in its trademarked motto: "Go Unnoticed."[6]

Effective cell tower camouflage doesn't only happen in the forest, desert, or suburban landscape. In cities, it can take the form of painting antenna panels the same color as the building façades they're mounted on, or hiding antennas around water towers, behind crenellations, or in cupolas or other architectural features on a rooftop. In the 2014 movie based on the Broadway musical *Annie*, the Daddy Warbucks character played by Jamie Foxx is a tech mogul and head of a cellular telephone company named William Stacks. In one scene Stacks takes Annie on a helicopter ride above New York City to show off all the cell towers his company "hide(s) in plain sight"—for example in the Statue of Liberty's crown—so his network can make good on its guarantee of total coverage. Flying low over a gothic cathedral, they swoop past a gargoyle on the roofline and Annie says, "Oh! I see a cell tower!" The mogul replies, "You know, Annie, sometimes what you're looking for . . . is right there in front of your face."

Daddy Stacks deliberately keeps his towers hidden. For security purposes, telecoms don't like to advertise the location of their towers, only the aggregate number of them: "Security Through Obscurity." The same goes for the actual workings of infrastructure. The Signal Space project, an independent research initiative by the architecture practice MKCA, with the purpose of "exploring the historical and contemporary relationships between broadcast technology and urban form," sums it up:

> Unlike the Empire State Building, Rockefeller Center, or other architectural landmarks of the broadcast infrastructure, the mobile phone infrastructure is a secret.

And even though its components are hidden in plain sight, its logics and workings are a mystery. This secrecy, and the limited opportunities for the public's input on the placement of antennas, coupled with anxiety about the effects of RF radiation exposure are reasons why people are so afraid of cell phone antennas.[7]

In response, the project is building a database linking to maps and visualizations representing the cellular infrastructure of New York City, in order to shed some light on the usually shadowy networks and to explore their implications for the future of cities.

Or suburbs. Local ordinances often affect the decision to disguise cell towers. Sometimes a fake tree is required in places where standards of taste and appearance are enforced, where homeowners' house paint, lawn care, fencing, and landscaping are determined by civic authority or the homeowners' association. On an autumn drive through the mountains of West Virginia, I tried to visit a giant cell tower camouflaged as a pine tree on the grounds of the famous Greenbrier resort and country club. I was stopped at the gate and politely turned away because I didn't have an appointment—just to drive a little way in and look at a cell tower from my car. The resort was built in 1913 by a railroad company and you still have to park across the road and (assuming you're allowed in) ride a tram back onto the grounds. The Greenbrier also has a large underground bunker, installed during the Cold War as a refuge from potential nuclear attack. Not entirely coincidentally, the bunker now houses a secure data center.

The 100-foot multiple-carrier tower on the property that I failed to see that day was designed to blend in with the tasteful environment of the resort, which is on the National Historic Registry. Ironically, one plan called for a real 75-foot pine to be cut down in order to make room for the fake tree.[8] Before it was built, a Verizon spokesperson told a local reporter more than the general public usually gets to hear about the actual crafting of a mono-pine tower: it would use "a detailed paint scheme with textured material to resemble the bark of a pine tree," and, as with an artificial Christmas tree, its branches were to be "attached to the pole with invisible wiring" and modeled on real pine branches, molded out of epoxy resin, with green plastic needles. The branches would be carefully placed "to shield the view of the antennas" closer to the trunk. The spokesperson jokes that the most serious problem they've faced is that "they look so realistic that squirrels keep chewing the needles off the branches." Never mind the fact that squirrels will also chew standard red or blue insulated electrical wires, we get it: owners of the expensive homes and guests of the resort will not be offended by the fake. And of course their cellphone service will improve significantly, along with that of many other Verizon customers in the area (other carriers were to be added later). The Greenbrier tree is a kind of luxury object, a bespoke tower. It took ten days to erect and cost $140,000, almost four times the cost of a standard tower at the time.[9] A photograph accompanying a follow-up news story confirms the effectiveness of the disguise. It looks pretty realistic, compared with other mono-pine towers I've seen.

I visited a more typical example in south Tampa, a 100-foot fake pine looming over a casual restaurant and its parking lot (Figure 4). The signs on the security fence alarmingly read, "do not climb tower without owners [*sic*]

FIGURE 4 Mono-pine tower in Tampa, Florida. Author's photograph.

written authorization!" (had this really been a problem, I wondered?), warned that "antennas may be active," and, next to a little radiating tower icon, dutifully disclaimed: "Beyond this point: Radio Frequency Fields at this site may exceed FCC rules for human exposure." An "ice-bridge" cable track protruded from the fat, brown, steel trunk, about seven feet up, where the cables emerged by way of a porthole. When I squinted up into the sunlight, I could see the dark-green plastic needles fluttering in the wind on branches arranged relatively artfully around the top of the pole to distract attention from the still-visible antennas. The needles made a whooshing sound not unlike the real Australian pines that are common in the area. But neither the branches nor the rigid trunk swayed in the wind, not even slightly, which was weird. When I left the site, I saw a newly installed white monopole a mile away, with no fake foliage and no visible antenna rack. The top section was opened up, the innards exposed, so I could see the long white panel antennas tucked in tightly, like three skinny caryatids standing shoulder to shoulder around a narrow column. With the top cover slid into place, the pole would be a seamless tube, like a giant cigarette stood on end. This is the opposite of the mono-pine strategy—make the tower so sleek and inoffensive it needn't actually try to hide.

A couple of months after I tried to visit the Greenbrier tree, I traveled to Colorado for a meeting, so I took the occasion to rent a car for some local cellspotting. Just outside Denver's dense population center, near the town of Ken Caryl, I saw a strange example of an exurban cell site, less luxurious than the Greenbrier pine, but also near large houses and equally intent on blending in. I pulled over just past one of the townhome developments that have sprung up everywhere at the edge of the foothills of the Rocky Mountains, to see what looked like the models for a tiny-house subdivision or the remnant of a miniature mall. An industrial park was visible further up the hill and a construction site was adjacent to the houses when I pulled over to take a closer look (though all was quiet on a Sunday). There are plenty of pseudo-traditional, wood-frame multistory buildings of this kind along America's highways, usually in housing developments or malls. But the odd proportions of these little buildings, and the fact that there were only four of them, alone, on a dirt road so close to the highway, made them stand out (Figure 5).

It turns out this was a little cellular Potemkin village, four uninhabited houses with wraparound porches and posts, all packed full of antennas and batteries and network equipment, with disproportionately tall cupolas, and windows that were light-opaque but radio-transparent. I had seen the site on RoadsideAmerica.com, where comments expressed reflexive nostalgia—"It makes you wonder how many real towns are left out there along America's highways"—but also macabre irony—"It's a peculiar little village, where there are no roads, no sidewalks, and nobody is ever there."[10] One user posted bleakly that the little houses looked like "replicas of tuberculosis huts from the late 1800s. It was then believed that people might be cured of tuberculosis by moving

FIGURE 5 Cellular village in Ken Caryl, Colorado. Author's photograph.

to a high, dry climate. The thin, dry air made it easier for those suffering from TB to breathe, but didn't cure any." Historically, there were indeed tuberculosis huts in nearby Colorado Springs, and these are perhaps what prompted the commenter's free-association (or dark joke). Maybe they also had in mind all the speculation about the potential health risks of radio frequency (RF) radiation, or the social isolation caused by excessive cellphone use.

That comment about the tuberculosis (TB) huts gets at something else significant about this cellular village: it feels haunted—more than a fake tree does—maybe because it's a fake human dwelling, a little ghost town. As the comment suggests, it's peculiar *because* "nobody is ever there." The site is practically a textbook illustration of Freud's theory of the uncanny—in German, *unheimlich*, meaning unhomely or alien, or weirdly familiar, but closely associated with its opposite term, *heimlich*, for that which is secret or kept in the home. Both can be creepy, but the ambiguous combination is the creepiest. That's the uncanny. Uncertainty is the heart of it. Although Freud ties the uncanny to castration anxiety (as he does most things) and the ultimate fear (of death), along the way he interprets the feeling in a more nuanced way, as the eerie sense we get from the return of something repressed—when something we deny as being part of ourselves emerges, as when in a horror movie we discover that the call is coming from *inside the house*. That's a later example, of course, but Freud's essay cites similar illustrations from folklore and literature, including automata, waxworks, puppets, doubles—all of which provoke uncertainty as to whether they're human or not, alive or not, real or not, in the home or not, us or not. He also notes the more literal homely/unhomely instance of the uncanny: a haunted house. The cellular village looks and feels like a set of tiny haunted houses, and you might say in this case that they are haunted by the innumerable disembodied voices and data that flow through them, information kept alive by antennas, wires, and batteries, relayed across the land through those little sheds, large enough for humans to be inside, perhaps, but not to live in. Nobody home—unless you count all that equipment, and the flow of powerful and invisible radio waves carrying streams of disembodied communications.

On the same road trip, I headed north toward the mountains and Yellowstone National Park. Near the Colorado-Wyoming border, at an elevation of about 6,000 feet, I spotted what from a distance looked like a big buffalo (or American bison) silhouetted on a hilltop off the side of Interstate 25 (Figure 6). When I got closer, I could see that

FIGURE 6 Cellular buffalo sculpture on the Terry Bison Ranch in Cheyenne, Wyoming. Author's photograph.

it was a flat cutout about 12 feet high—or, actually, two cutouts making a kind of thin sandwich, mounted on either side of a rack with three posts and a crossbar sunk into the rocky hill, the whole thing like a buffalo-shaped billboard. I've seen similar metal silhouettes mounted on fences and barns in rural regions across America—cowboys, horses, a soldier. The buffalo is the official mascot of the University of Colorado, where I'd just been for my meeting, and you see it printed everywhere on flags and sports paraphernalia in a similar silhouette, so I might have assumed that this sculpture was a tribute by an avid football fan. Maybe that's how it was originally created. But I was on the lookout for this landmark, which I had seen on the internet, along with its GPS coordinates. I could see four long cellular antennas on each side, painted black and bracketed onto the metal body like electromagnetic ribs. Viewed head-on as I passed, the bison looked more like a conventional cell tower: the shape of the animal disappeared, and the antennas stuck out on both sides of the upright post. It looked like a simple monopole tower, with antenna panels and cables running down the frame supporting the sculpture. Looking back at the tower as I passed, I saw the buffalo again, and I also spotted a small white microwave drum on a short pole, like a little round calf trailing a few yards behind, no doubt used for backhaul to a switching station. The cellular buffalo is a flat representation of the real animal you can see in grazing herds in that part of the country, along with cattle, pronghorn antelope, elk, and other species of commercial livestock and free-range wildlife. Nearby Yellowstone National Park hosts the largest herd of bison in the United States. When I got there the next day, my rental car was blocked by a slowly passing herd, a typical experience for tourists driving through the park. One big buffalo nearly bumped my sideview mirror.

The buffalo cell tower stands on the edge of the Terry Bison Ranch (27,500 acres), a working livestock business (Horseshoe Bison, Inc.) coupled with an agritourist resort and roadside attraction.[11] Lists of American roadside attractions along the interstate highways tend to emphasize the weird and the kitsch. People head to them in the spirit of nostalgic-ironic adventure. They often include novelty buildings or sculptures—a giant concrete dinosaur, or a line of half-buried Cadillacs. Hand-painted billboards and other signage, sometimes in a recognizably and often self-consciously "primitive" or "outsider" style, are also part of the aesthetic. Terry Bison Ranch calls itself a "western adventure resort," with cabins, campsites, gift shop, recreational vehicle (RV) park, mock-up old-West town, horseback tours, pony rides, and a train you can ride out onto the range to view and hand-feed some of the 2,500 head of real buffalo. One hand-painted sign marks a "Prehistoric Buffalo Chip (over 5,000 years old)." The ranch goes back to the nineteenth century and Teddy Roosevelt slept there (twice). The ranch was named for its 1887 owner, Charles Terry, but the current owners, the Thiel family, added the roadside attraction in an entrepreneurial spirit during the 1990s.

When I got to the ranch, I ordered a draft beer and a bison burger in the Brass Buffalo Saloon. The bartender told me that the owner, Ron Thiel, was the sculptor who cut and welded the metal buffalo. Driving in I had seen several smaller metal buffaloes, airplanes, and other sculptures mounted on posts and gates, and there seemed to be a series of large welded crosses up on another ridge. Thiel was trained as an engineer, and he also built the ranch's old-fashioned train, children's playground rides, and a small suspension bridge. Verizon first approached the ranch in the 1990s about leasing tower space on the bison sculpture, which was already mounted on the hilltop, waiting to be wired.

As a symbol, the buffalo is overdetermined (to say the least). That is, it has many possible contributing sources and invokes a range of conflicting historical meanings. As the ranch's website reminds us, the US Congress passed the National Bison Legacy Act in April 2016, acknowledging that the animal is "a historical symbol of the United States" and officially naming it the "national mammal," while also noting that bison "were integrally linked with the economic and spiritual lives of many Indian tribes through trade and sacred ceremonies."[12] The bison still plays a central role in art and traditional ceremonies of some tribes, in which dancers wear the head and skin of the buffalo, for example. On the other hand, for some the bison signifies the myth of the American West, the frontier, the idea of manifest destiny, a settler ideology. Finally, and consequently, the species has become a symbol of conservation, a reminder of the rapacious devastation of natural resources by settlers, and the connection of that devastation to genocidal wars against indigenous peoples. It's easy, especially for those of us not living in the western states, to forget that the bison is both a real animal and a deeply conflicted symbol.

The ranch's mission statement includes an imperative: "Make guests believe they have participated in a new western adventure that sparks the imagination." The website notes the importance of buffalo to Native Americans, but it doesn't point out that the species was hunted to near-extinction, sometimes as part of campaigns to drive into reservations or exterminate the Native American peoples who depended on it as a food source. The colorful, old-fashioned train that visitors can ride to the herd, from which they can reach out to feed vitamin pellets to the shaggy animals, inevitably invokes nineteenth-century railways from which hunters fired rifles at much larger free-range herds. The buffalo silhouette on the hill makes me think of all of this, of everything concealed behind the image of the American Bison—and of the Native American hunting technique in which a human concealed himself in a buffalo skin in order to lead the herd over a cliff.

The Terry Bison Ranch is a business. It made a deal with Verizon in the same entrepreneurial spirit with which it opened the roadside attraction in the 1990s. And the telecom presumably leased the metal buffalo for a tower primarily because it was already well-situated on its hill and provided localized, ready-made camouflage. But that doesn't mean that the parties to the deal would have been blind to all the buffalo symbolism. The myth of the frontier has long been exploited by cellular telecom companies. The expansion of towers across the nation into hitherto "unsettled" or uncovered regions has been part of business models and sales pitches for years. Telecoms have historically competed over who has the best coverage, but as recent media ads admit, coverage is now pretty close to the same for most carriers, at least in populated regions.

The steel bison isn't really a copy of an actual animal—except maybe for that brief moment it fools the eye as we approach from a distance. It's a copy of a symbol, or a whole set of symbols and competing myths, and, inadvertently, a reminder of a conflicted history: native culture, settler ideology, old-West adventure, hunting, ranching, railroads, mass extinction, genocide. The cellular buffalo is folk art, kin to all those roadside billboards out there ("See Rock City"), but it also smuggles technology in its flattened form. The rib-antennas are hidden not on a fake animal, but on a fake billboard shaped like a mythic animal. Ultimately, the buffalo is another roadside attraction, meant to "[m]ake guests believe." So it's appropriate that it uses misdirection, P. T. Barnum-style, when it comes to the magic of cellular telephony: "Giant infrastructure! Made to disappear before your very eyes!" Just as ironic travelers seek out concrete dinosaurs and authentic mid-century diners alongside the highway, some now seek out the cellular buffalo (I'm one of them). The irony of the technology behind the façade becomes another part of the roadside experience.

Camouflaged cell towers in general—whether fake pine trees, palm trees, cacti, rocks, clock towers, flagpoles, or steeples—are more than practical solutions to the NIMBY (Not In My Back Yard) problem. They're often awkward manifestations of shared cultural assumptions about the natural world, conflicting histories, religious iconography, and also the collective desire for invisible and ethereal connectivity—which is mixed up with many of those assumptions and with the messy materiality of the actual networks they supposedly help conceal. Most of all, stealth towers camouflage infrastructure. No wonder the results seem so weird. There's a lot going on behind their thin disguises.

4 ETHEREAL CONNECTIONS

Many once believed in an invisible substance permeating the atmosphere: the ether. The word literally means "upper air," but the term "ethereal" connotes presences there, spirits, immaterial forces traveling above our material, mundane existence. It was once thought that radio waves were propagated via the ether. We still send data over ethernet connections, though ethereal connotations are more often attached to the tricks we do wirelessly, via Wi-Fi, Bluetooth, or cellular networks. And Ether is the name of a cryptocurrency on the Ethereum blockchain-based platform, a new kind of dematerialization trick. Similarly, popular ideas of the cloud assume that it's some sort of airy medium in the sky, when it's really just someone else's computer—actually, some company's warehouse full of computers, racks of servers humming away day and night, always in danger of overheating.

Many still imagine the cellular network as an ethereal thing—airy, immaterial, indistinguishable from magic. The

150-foot cell tower, bolted down to concrete footers, is an imposing material object, but it often carries oddly ethereal connotations, as if it were a portal for invisible forces traveling through the air. Come to think of it, it sort of is. Maybe that's why we're surprised when we see the outer shell removed from a simple monopole tower. It's not the smooth, featureless mast it appears to be: it's full of tangled entrails! On some level we know this, but most of the time we think of such towers as giant magic wands for conjuring voices and data through invisible radiation. When you see it being installed, a stealth flagpole, say, reveals that its narrow white trunk is actually stuffed full of cables and wrapped around with close arrays of oblong-panel antennas, as well as smaller boxes used for amplification or wireless relay down to the ground where the base station sits. The smooth pole is just a façade. When you see a mono-pine tower up close it spoils an illusion you didn't know you were entertaining, especially when you see an open porthole near the base of the trunk with exposed cables spilling out.

I found those last two images, of an exposed flagpole and an eviscerated mono-pine, on the website of a firm specializing in telecommunications law, including leases, regulations, towers, and other infrastructure.[1] The site's image gallery includes a variety of camouflaged towers: flagpoles, light poles, boulders, pine trees (like the ones at Greenbrier and in Tampa), palm trees, eucalyptus trees, cacti, clock towers, water towers, billboards, lighthouses, silos, windmills, a Motel 6 sign, a McDonalds sign, an Outback

Steakhouse sign, the buffalo sculpture I saw in Wyoming, brick chimneys, adobe houses, rooftop cupolas, abstract sculptural obelisks, a surprising number of church spires, steeples, bell towers, and giant crosses. Now, I don't want to make too much of this last set of religious-property cell sites. Churches have to pay the rent and pay for physical-plant repairs, utility bills, and cable and internet connections. The offer of a lease from a telecom is surely welcome. A spire is an ancient form of tower from which bells are rung, to convey time or other information. In the case of Islam, a minaret is a tower from which the mu'adhdhin issues the call to prayer. The association of such sacred towers with telephony makes sense in that larger context. A logical convergence of practicality and cultural symbolism connects steeples and cell towers. The traditional architectural iconography of spiritual aspiration, vertical structures reaching for the heavens, already shares something with the need to lift antennas up high into the air in order to get in touch with invisible energies. Call it a convergence of etherealities, two kinds of conduits for different kinds of otherworldly forces, cellular infrastructure and religious architecture.

But it still feels a little weird when we open the steeple and see . . . a cell tower, as we do in a video tour posted by a vlogger with the handle MrMobile.[2] The video lets us follow an AT&T installation of a complete cell site inside a Unitarian church steeple in Duxbury, Massachusetts (est. 1840). The carrier was interested in the site primarily for its height and constructed an entirely new, translucent fiberglass replacement steeple to house the technology. The new material is light-translucent and radio-transparent. From the inside, the steeple has an otherworldly glow. Upstairs, the host says, "you find more cables than any church should need." We follow him up a narrow staircase to the tower, where a giant bell still rings, then up a ladder into the steeple itself. MrMobile says, "this is where the magic happens," then lets us hear the evidence of radio magic—a badly shielded camera hums eerily in response to radio frequency (RF) energy in the steeple as the operator pans to the standard orange warning sign: "Beyond this point radio frequency fields at this site exceed the FCC rules for human exposure," with a little cell tower icon with semicircular radio waves emanating from it. We're told that the congregation will be safe, since they'll sit directly beneath the outwardly radiating energy and at a distance that leverages the inverse square law for the exponential drop-off of RF radiation as you move away from the source. The video segment ends out back in a concrete shelter containing the switching equipment, a rack of batteries, and a big generator.

One point of the segment is that "keeping people happy meant refitting half a church," by which I think the host means that finding an aesthetically pleasing and religiously acceptable solution that would still meet the needs of the site required an effort: keeping the people at AT&T happy, as well as the congregation, and, incidentally, the budget committee. You can detect in his voice, and in the earlier joke about seeing so much cable in a church, a hint of the irony many would perceive in what looks like an unholy union of commercial technology and spiritual architecture. But, as I said, such deals represent a logical meeting of different ideas of the ethereal: one sacred and one profane, one accessed through a portal to invisible spiritual forces and one by transceiving invisible radio signals, both requiring similar infrastructures. This precise conjunction was noticed by one artist who participated in an online "Paint A Cell Tower" challenge in 2018. Joshua Davis posted a photo of his painting, "Steeples," which depicts a latticework cell tower next to a different church steeple, both tower and steeple set against a glowing blue and yellow sky. The artist commented: "I loved how the light was filtered in the steeple window. I also love the idea of the cell tower being a steeple and the steeple being a communications tower of sorts . . ."[3] Bringing voices into proximity, providing a sense of presence, annihilating distance, putting people in touch with higher powers, communicating with things unseen—all of this could describe either the church building or the cell site. It stands to reason they are sometimes found in combination.

One company, SteepleCom (http://www.steeplecom. com), calls itself "advocates for churches in the wireless age." It specializes in helping churches broker deals with telecoms to install cell sites on their properties. Promotional materials say that a steeple is "a tall pre-existing structure," and therefore a "natural fit" for antennas, and that such deals are a way to direct revenues to "those that do good works." Comments on the company's YouTube channel, however, accuse it of "poison[ing] people with emf waves while they go to pray to God," and warn conspiratorially that the United Nations (UN) "will use this towers [*sic*] against them very soon," ending with a citation from the Book of Revelation.

The apotheosis of the combination of religious iconography with cellular technology may be the cell tower disguised as a cross. There's a striking example near my university in Tampa, Florida, on the grounds of the New Life Tabernacle Church (Figure 7). The cross stands out at

FIGURE 7 Cellular cross in Tampa, Florida. Author's photograph.

the edge of church property near the northbound lanes of Highway Interstate-75. At about 150 feet, it's much taller than the palm trees along the road, and it glows bright white against the blue sky. However, a few miles south on the highway you pass a tall, fat flagpole with a very different kind of symbol hanging from it, a larger-than-life Confederate battle flag. The flag's theatrically big, 30 feet by 50 feet, at one time claiming the dubious distinction of being the largest Confederate flag in the world. The owner raised it in 2008 on a private patch of land, a park approved by the county before it knew the flag would fly there. It's lost on no one that it went up the year Barack Obama was elected the first African American president of the United States. Numerous protesters and the mayor of Tampa have called for its removal. The Facebook page dedicated to the flag features racist, sexist, anti-government posts, including one photo with the MLK Boulevard exit sign in the background. The flag is an unfortunate geographical coincidence for the church just a few miles north. But some see the cellular cross as providing a positive answer to the hateful flag, I was told.[4]

From the highway, the cross looks bright white and thin, almost delicate. Up close at the cell site, which is located between a grassy soccer field and a retaining pond, the steel poles look grayish and a little weathered. The tubular upright is enormous, bolted together in three large segments and slightly faceted. I know that the top is packed with antennas, amplifiers, relays, and cables. Standing close to the tower and looking up, I can see large ventilation holes in the upper segment and a small lightning rod sticking out from the very top, too fine to be visible from the highway. (Tampa is supposedly the lightning capital of North America.) The day I stopped I got lucky: a technician opened the gate and let me walk inside the security fence to look around at the ground space, a rare privilege, where I saw a freshly poured concrete slab for a second carrier, T-Mobile, soon to be co-located there. (The current lease is with Verizon.) This will require an additional set of equipment, including a new tier of antennas inside the cross, and new cables to join the existing red, green, and blue bunches that now emerge from a low porthole and run across the ice bridge (as they call it) to the switching box. That day, the new backhaul cable was already buried in a trench with fresh dirt on top, headed underground toward the nearest network switching station. A metal cabinet contained a rack of eight batteries, and a propane tank was hooked up to the existing generator. The new T-Mobile generator will run on diesel that will supposedly last longer during power outages.

For an evangelical Christian church like this one, a prominent cross is already an act of communication (as the artist implied about the steeple he painted), a kind of spiritual semaphore. The pastor told me the congregation fully supported the construction of the cross for this reason, but some local residents outside the church telephoned to complain that the money for construction should have gone to feed the hungry instead.[5] From his point of view, Verizon's approaching the church was providential. He quoted the bible verse, "the children of the world are often wiser than the children of light" (Luke 16:8), to say that the church has to market itself in order to reach the community. And of course, as he might have added (but did not), the lease provided welcome income. A cellphone video of the cross on YouTube, made from a moving car on the highway, features a conspiracy-minded passenger or driver who says that in her opinion the cross-tower is used for mind control.[6] (She may well have been connected to that very tower when recording her video.) An online comment raises a fair question: "Is it your opinion that cell towers are used for mind control? Or that the control in this case was the masking of the true intent of that structure i.e. feigning appearance of a religious symbol rather than transcieving [*sic*] wireless data signals?"

The idea that spirituality and technology might overlap has deep roots. Arthur C. Clarke's famous observation that any sufficiently advanced technology is indistinguishable from magic seems especially relevant to cellular networks.[7] In this case, the magic begins with a disappearing trick that makes infrastructure vanish before our very eyes. There's a long history of treating the electromagnetic spectrum as a medium for unseen worlds and occult knowledge, since it makes possible connections that seem to defy time and space. Metaphors about networks being haunted and referring to ghostly voices in the ether are not only metaphors—they're verbal remnants of a century-old tradition. "Because we live in a physical world," some once thought, "denizens of the spiritual world would need some kind of natural force to cross over to our realm," and radio waves might be that force or medium.[8] Because electromagnetic energy acts beyond our senses, and because the "extrasensory parts of the electromagnetic spectrum form more and more of our artifactual environment," a radio object like the cell tower can seem like a portal to another dimension, a gateway for otherworldly forces.[9]

So-called whistler hunters make a hobby of listening to the airwaves for naturally generated radio signals, which can be caused by a whole range of atmospheric phenomena.[10] These enthusiasts often do their listening in remote places where radio noise is reduced to a minimum. They hear faint sounds in their headphones when they pick up the waves, clicks and pops and long eerie whistles like the sound of a warbly theremin, a musical instrument you play by waving your hands between two RF antennas.[11] Anthony Dunne says that the appeal of these sounds for some whistler hunters is "quasi-mystical," and for others it's "a defiant gesture against people's careless attitude toward nature."[12] Others pursue what they call electronic voice phenomena (EVP). Historically, some of the first listeners to voices on the phonograph when it was new believed they were hearing the devil or demons from another world. EVP enthusiasts continue in this general tradition, intentionally listening for voices of the dead, interdimensional beings, or alien presences, aurally camouflaged in static hiss, or captured on audiotape, submerged in ambient noise, in any case, requiring a leap of faith or apophenia—the perception of patterns among random phenomena (the clinical version of which is paranoia).[13]

Early understanding of radio often relied on analogies from metaphysics. Technologies that tap into the electromagnetic spectrum have invited paranormal (or paranoid) explanations from their earliest discovery, already evident in the experiments of Marconi and Tesla, for example. Thomas Edison himself drew up designs for what he called a spirit phone, a device for talking to the dead. Today you can download EVP apps for your smartphone, one of which is named Ethereal.[14] For most enthusiasts, the hardware and software are just a means to a spiritualist end. They're interested in the immaterial realm, whether manifest through digital app, magnetic tape, or metal antenna. Both radio spiritualism and the worry that RF radiation causes cancer, for example, tend to gloss over the mundane workings of the system of conveyance, particularly the infrastructure. Cement, cables, steel, batteries, generators, conduits, and antennas are less amenable than the ethereal spectrum is to belief in things unseen. In this context, cell towers, sources of invisible radiation, often retain a bit of the aura of the paranormal once associated with early radio.

Such feelings provide the premise for Stephen King's horror novel, *Cell*, published in 2006, just before the appearance of the iPhone.[15] Writing just a few years after 9/11, at a moment of the then-high point in the adoption of mobile phones, King imagines an apocalypse set in motion when everyone who puts a cellphone to their ear hears a mysterious Pulse, an encoded audio signal that fries their brain and turns them into a zombie, or, as characters in the novel say, a "phone-crazy" or "phoner." The novel builds on the anti-cellphone culture panic already underway at the time, which traded in clichés about people being turned into zombies by using their Blackberries (a corporate joke called them Crackberries) and flip phones. What if it were literally true, King must have thought. The author's bio for the novel ends in this case with the declaration that "[h]e does not own a cell phone." And a teacher-character in the novel (sounding a bit like *The Simpsons*' Ned Flanders) refers to cellphones as the "devil's intercoms."[16]

As in any good zombie story, the normies of *Cell* have to kill lots of the undead on their journey in order to survive, and there's plenty of terror generated around the mindlessness of the afflicted. The blunt title presumably refers to the common short name for a cellphone. But what's especially interesting is that the deeper source of horror remains largely offstage until the end: the cell towers and the cellular network they support. "They saw we had built the Tower of Babel all over again . . . and on nothing but electronic cobwebs. And in a space of seconds, they brushed those cobwebs aside and our Tower fell."[17] In a mixed metaphor, the biblical Tower of Babel, the ancient symbol of hubris and scrambled communications, is built on the cobweb-network of cell towers.

The destructive Pulse works like an online virus via an audible executable file. King seems to have imagined it as something like the encoded bleeps of a dial-up modem, which had long driven people crazy with annoyance and had only recently been displaced by broadband access. The Pulse comes from somewhere unseen or from everywhere at once, as in this speculative exposition:

> "I suppose the right genius could hack the wrong satellite signal into all those microwave towers you see . . . the ones that boost the signals along . . ."
>
> Clay knew the towers he was talking about, steel skeletons with dishes stuck all over them like gray suckers. They had popped up everywhere over the last ten years.[18]

Latticework microwave towers are like an army of giant steel skeletons straight out of classic space-invasion films. The most frightening part seems to be how they had popped up everywhere in just a decade. On the surface, King's is a broadcast model of terror. A single source emanates from an unknown location, maybe a hacker's garage or terrorist's safe house, with effects reminiscent of the panic-inducing radio announcements in the 1938 broadcast, *War of the Worlds*. But the deeper terror in the novel comes from following out the implications of the invisible wireless network, distributed over innumerable hexagonal cells across the face of the Earth. What if disembodied sounds carried destructive occult power everywhere, all at once, via such a global cobweb? The literally explosive denouement takes place via a *deus ex machina*: a pirate cell tower, mounted in a dead zone atop a disused parachute-drop ride by rogue carnival workers. The protagonists suddenly get three bars thanks to the rigged-up tower, so they're able to use their one phone to detonate a bus-bomb that kills a horde of phoner zombies. The victims die (again) because of a cell tower.

As writer Kristen Gallerneaux says, every new communication medium, from the telegraph to the telephone, has come with deepening anxieties and, paradoxically, with an increased desire for contact with the ineffable, including the dead and the afterlife. In her view "the collisions between belief, reproduction, and creativity became permanently altered" in response to these new technologies, as distances between persons were reduced while consciousness was opened up, extended into unseen dimensions.[19] Gallerneaux provides a number of strange historical examples that go beyond familiar media platforms, including the World War I Chief Signal Officer for the US Army, George Owen Squier, who discovered that he could use headphones to listen in on the Germans' encrypted wireless telegraph transmissions by hooking antenna wires to the tops of tall trees in the forest, an application straight out of Grimm's *Tales* and anticipating the weirdness of camouflaged cell towers.[20] For many, all those cell towers out there feel a little like that signal-haunted forest. Antennas are spooky things. They can close vast distances and let you hear invisible, disembodied voices, then automatically drop your connection and hand you off to the next tower, and the next. We may flatter ourselves that our demystified understanding has outrun primitive visceral responses like those of EVP enthusiasts or pseudo scientific whistler hunters, but something of a haunted feeling still clings to the growing forest of cellular towers that quietly engulfs us a little more each day. As Gallerneaux shows, that World War I radio engineer who deployed the sneaky "tree telephony" was associated with the invention of telecom multiplexing in 1910, a way to share multiple signals over a single channel or cable. And he also invented, in 1922, a method for piping in soothing disembodied musical voices via electrical wiring—that is, the vaguely creepy, arguably undead (since revenant easy-listening covers are the most common genre), ubiquitous soundtrack of modern life patented as Muzak. Nowadays, public background music is usually supplied by internet streaming services, often over wireless speakers connected via radio waves.[21]

5 DESIGN

Who designs cell towers? After the era of heroic telecommunication towers like the ones discussed in Chapter 2, the more utilitarian towers of today's broadcast and cellular systems came from a different place, culturally—from civil engineering and specialty construction companies rather than architects. There are patent drawings on file, of course, but they don't emphasize the aesthetics of such objects. There are exceptions to the distinction between the two kinds of design, like monumental bridges, for example, feats of engineering that are also sometimes prestige projects for architects. But like highway signs, bridges, sewer tunnels, traffic lights, streetlights, and power-line pylons, cell towers are standardized pieces of infrastructure, although, in the United States, at least, they're owned by commercial companies and usually located on leased parcels of private land. Innovations, like sleek monopoles as an alternative to latticework towers, are introduced from time to time, but the range of designs remains limited, for practical reasons.

The rare exception proves the rule. Remember that cell tower in the form of a giant white cross? About 50 miles east of it on Interstate 4, near the busy entrance to Disney World, you can see a 100-foot power-line pylon in the abstract shape of a Mickey Mouse head—three proportioned circles made of fat steel tubes, a large one for the head and two smaller ones for the ears. It was commissioned by the Tampa Electric Company to feed electrical power to the sprawling entertainment complex. The abstract head of The Mouse was designed by Disney artists, who incorporated laser-driven fiber-optic illumination at night. This is a rare collaboration between a power company and an entertainment corporation. There are a handful of other examples of creative or fanciful designs for power-line stanchions or pylons,[1] but most of them are pre-engineered towers based on one of several common designs.

Like power-line pylons, cell towers are mostly adapted from established plans and specifications, designed by anonymous contractors and staff engineers. In other words, they're the result of a typical industrial design process, utilitarian objects optimized for mass distribution and installation with minimum fuss, with their form determined by their function. Companies that specialize in camouflaged or stealth towers naturally employ visual artists to design and sculpt their various disguises: pine-tree branches or epoxy-resin bark applied to the steel trunk, or the architectural housing for a bell tower or a suburban clock tower. In rare cases a folk artist like the ranch owner in Wyoming who made the cellular buffalo becomes an ad hoc collaborator with the tower company and the telecom. Such special cases help us to understand the much more common practice when it comes to infrastructural objects on this scale. These big, intrusive objects are usually designed to be spawned in large numbers across the environment while, as far as possible, remaining in the background.

The most designed aspect of the user's experience of the cellular network is the app in the miniature smartphone interface, especially those familiar little bars or dots, the Received Signal Strength Indicator (RSSI). The graphical icon with its row of ascending bars looks like a tiny silhouetted skyline or a miniature histogram chart. It's usually located near the logo of the carrier you're hoping to connect to, and near that other familiar icon, the dot with emanating arcs representing your Wi-Fi connectivity. On my current iPhone (running iOS 12), four bars filled-in or grayed-out represent the relative strength of my cellular signal. (Approximately.) Apple returned to a bars icon with iOS 11, after a period (iOS 7 to iOS 10) in which signal strength was indicated with a row of five dots. Other makes of phone have varied the graphic motif, some using five bars instead of four, for example.

Graphical signal strength icons go back to the earliest cell phones in the 1980s, and most people are at least vaguely aware that they're just a visual metaphor, only an approximate representation of the actual radio frequency (RF) signal. As everyone knows, you can see one or two bars darkened and still not have a connection, because of interference from surrounding buildings, for example, or a heavy call load on the nearest tower. You can choose to see a more precise decibel-milliwatts (dBm) measurement of your signal displayed in numbers by dialing a string of characters and switching your phone to field test mode, but most users never get to know about this option. The bars, reaching up a little higher as each is filled in left to right, vaguely remind us of those unseen towers we hope to ping. It's satisfying in a familiar way when you get more bars. That small comforting response is an example of what Donald Norman (who once worked for Apple) calls emotional design, which, he argues, "may be more critical to a product's success than its practical elements."[2] To appeal to users in this way, to have an emotional effect while also serving a useful purpose, takes both "the skills of the visual and graphic artist and the industrial engineer."[3] If you raise your eyes from your phone and look at the large object on the horizon, it's clear: consumer electronics may be designed with aesthetics and emotional response in mind but cell towers usually are not.

The closest most cell towers get to deploying emotional design is the trickery of camouflage, and usually this produces unintended emotional responses of anger or disgust. Mark Favermann, an alumnus of Harvard's Graduate School of Design, argues that telecom companies and governments should just skip the camouflage and "hire or commission sculptors to create the cell phone structures as interesting pieces of public art."[4] This would both improve public relations for the companies and enhance the built environment. He's seen this approach in Italy, he says, where cell towers have been "designed as beautiful structures themselves," their forms "created by architects, industrial designers and sculptors." Favermann's own designs include a speculative prototype named the Call Angel, a kind of updated phone kiosk for making video calls (I can't tell from the drawings whether these would take place via Wi-Fi, fiber-optic internet, or cellular connection). The Call Angel is a 7-foot pole with a small (2–3 foot) folded canopy of solar-panel wings on top, LED lighting running down the sides of the pole, a screen, camera, and speaker, as well as a card reader for taking payment.[5]

When he praises Italian design, Favermann seems to have in mind in particular the Calzavara company of Rome and Basiliano. The firm says it aims to supply "innovative infrastructures," high-end camouflaged towers, including fake pine trees and palm trees and—this being Italy—cypresses, as well as cells on wheels (COWs), portable, temporary, self-contained cell sites that can be brought in during a natural disaster or other emergency, or in support of a large public event.[6] But their most distinctive products are towers meant to combine aesthetics with engineering, especially the so-called mosaic tower model.[7] One striking installation stands 100 feet tall in the Piazza Giacomo Matteotti in Treviso (Figure 8). The tower has a triangular cross-section, echoing the shape of the piazza itself, which also serves as a car park and sometimes hosts a tented market. It's across the street from a museum in a former monastery associated with the fourteenth-century church of Santa Caterina, near a section of the old Roman wall.

FIGURE 8 Murano mosaic tower, on the Piazza G. Matteotti, in Treviso, Italy, Pamio Design for Calzavara SPA. Photo courtesy Calzavara.

Some of the tower's base-station equipment is installed in a room below the museum. A traditional stone campanile (bell tower) stands just to the west. This version of the mosaic tower was designed by the Pamio Design firm to cover the structural skeleton provided by Calzavara's engineers. It's sheathed with an astonishing 500,000 16 mm tiles made of

Murano glass (Venice and Murano are about 25 miles away). In daylight, diagonal patterns of tiny tiles shine blue, green, and gold. At night, the tower, illuminated from within by LEDs, sheds colored light down the narrow streets extending from the piazza.

When I checked on Google Earth (summer 2019), a gold scooter was parked next to the tower and a few cars were parked around it in the piazza. The tower had been tagged by graffiti writers and there were tape marks where paper flyers had been removed from its shiny metal base. In many world cities, you'll find similar graffiti and posted flyers on public statues and pillars. But Italy—Rome, in particular— has a very old tradition of posting political or social satires (*pasquinades*) on a statue (nicknamed Pasquino) in a public square, using it as a kind of community bulletin board.[8] Contemporary Romans keep up the tradition self-consciously, sticking posters and flyers on several statues around the ancient capital city. On the one hand, the tower in Treviso is just another urban surface on which to post flyers or write graffiti (*e allora?* as the Italians say—so what?). On the other hand, the Pasquino is called a talking statue, because of the printed-text voices that appear on it. The Murano mosaic tower is a talking statue in a different sense, a sculpture that serves as a relay for voices and data. The graffiti and flyers on its base may be a way for some local residents to talk back to the talking obelisk, a way to re-mark the territory of the piazza as not entirely under the control of the phone company whose equipment is concealed in the tower.

This cellular obelisk is described by the manufacturer as "urban street furniture," which will enable clients to participate in the data-gathering trends known as the Internet of Things (IoT) and the Smart City. The metal panel on the base, above the flyers and graffiti, is etched with an official warning (in Italian): "MONITORED VIDEO SYSTEM." The talking sculpture is watching you, and maybe listening to you, as well. Optional features for the mosaic tower include IoT sensors and video surveillance cameras. There's even a line of third-party designer video cameras available that look like cute cartoon animals—grasshoppers, birds, iguanas—that can be mounted as if they were clinging to the edge of the tower (none of these animal cameras was installed on the Treviso tower). The firm that makes the animal cameras explicitly markets them as camouflaged emotional designs. The iguana looking down at you replaces the "intimidating effect" and "'looming control'" of video surveillance cameras, substituting a cute and "playful" object instead, one that nonetheless "conceals an 'intelligent' artificial vision technology that guarantees high performance."[9]

Calzavara offers a different modular kiosk system explicitly for smart city solutions, without a cell tower component but with other technology inside, called the Dicecell.[10] It consists of triangular blocks that can be stacked in various multicolored configurations. Each block contains a module providing a different service: Wi-Fi routers, environmental sensors, Bluetooth beacons, clocks, solar panels, cellphone chargers, video surveillance cameras.

The audio for the online slideshow about the system plays a techno track with siren sound effects: "*Nobody rules these streets at night like me.*" When I looked at the brochure, use cases were dominated by images of Chinese installations, an ominous sign at a time when China is building a total-surveillance infrastructure for its universal social-credit system, combining facial recognition and personal data in order to identify, reward, and punish citizens, and persecute the Muslim Uyghur people, for example, as well as journalists and political dissidents.

Design is never purely aesthetic. It often has designs on us. The visually pleasing decorated kiosks and sculptural cell towers can literally conceal other motives and functions beyond simple personal communication. Infrastructure, conceptually running beneath the technologies with which we interact directly, is never entirely neutral. It's the product of specific interests and assumptions, some of which get baked in and some of which (sometimes literally, as in the case of the animal cameras) attach themselves after installation. In the case of cell towers, the illusions of invisibility, immateriality, and ubiquity can themselves be harnessed in the service of powerful interests beyond those of the commercial tower companies and telecoms.

For all of its modularity and colorful surface effects, the Torre Matteotti relies on a fairly conventional skeleton—a triangular cross-section made of steel poles with diagonal trusses. Structurally, this is a typical cell tower. What might a cell tower look like if a designer started from scratch? There have been some experiments with non-towers—balloons, drones, even satellites—for lifting up antennas, but what about rethinking the material basis of the tower itself? One speculative design has done just that. Its creator, Skylar Tibbits, is founder and co director of MIT's Self-Assembly Lab, which conducts experiments in programmable and self-assembling materials. The lab builds objects that semi-automatically take new forms when stimulated by heat, water, light, or the kinetic energy from being agitated or tumbled. This research began as a response to the question of how to get 3D-printed objects assembled once their components were manufactured. That's why Tibbits calls this aspect of the Lab's work 4D printing: 3D plus the dimension of time. Objects are printed, then, when prompted, they self-assemble into programmed forms.[11]

So far, most of these have been demos or proofs of concept, shaken up or tumbled around until their pieces find one another and connect into a geometric whole, or heated until they curl up and close like origami animals into pre designed shapes. It's a method for treating basic materials as programmable, using digital tools in combination with physical stuff to make things that turn themselves into other things.[12] Sandwich-like combinations of materials with different properties can result in textiles that curl when cut or bubble up in tufted textures. Or braided or woven shapes can morph in response to a simple stimulus, a temperature change, or a human pulling on one thread, like working a flexible marionette.

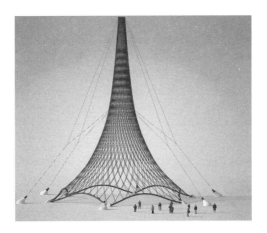

FIGURE 9 Speculative cell tower design by Skylar Tibbits for *The New York Times Magazine*. Illustration courtesy Justin Metz.

That last example, of textile-like, braided or woven designs, was the basis of Tibbits's entry in a speculative design challenge sponsored by *The New York Times,* a charge to rethink everyday objects in radically new ways—in his case cell towers, which, a reporter points out with ironic understatement, normally "aren't handsome things."[13] Instead of employing the strategy of camouflaging the cell tower as something else, or wrapping it in an aesthetically pleasing skin, Skylar Tibbits reimagined the essential structure of the tower itself (Figure 9). The result looks like a giant upside-down funnel-shaped 3D data visualization. He asked, "How can we make it change shape, bend, twist, twirl, expand, so the cell tower can adjust to the weather, time of use, time of day—or if there's a big event nearby?" The Self-Assembly Lab had already experimented with a few large-scale objects of this sort. For example, they built 60-foot towers as scaffolding for concerts or other arena performances, big wide-mouthed see-through pylons made of responsive fibers. The result looks like one of those toy finger-cuffs, woven from paper strands that grip tighter when pulled—but for a giant. One video shows researchers in a warehouse raising a tower by pulling on slim guy-wires, as if they were handling a big balloon for the Macy's Thanksgiving Day parade, until it sways high over their heads but remains light and manageable, which they demonstrate by manipulating it in various ways like a huge puppet.[14] Even larger towers could be built in this way, consisting of what amounts to macro-scale textiles, biaxially braided woven forms. They could stretch and reshape in uncanny dances (like those skinny inflated "air dancers" flapping around outside malls and car dealerships), and they could be manipulated by a single human operator (or other force) pulling on a thread. That thread would actually be as thick as a cable, a tube made of composite fiberglass or carbon fiber, with multiple such threads braided together in a predesigned pattern: "Small forces at the base of the structure—heat, wind, even an electronic signal—could affect large transformations up above," as Tibbits explains. Reconfigurable cell towers could be stronger and more flexible, automatically morphing, hunkering down in response to extreme weather, for example, or stretching up in response to increased demand for connections. But Tibbits also mentions the benefit of emotional design, a responsive aspect of their appeal: "the tower can dance; the tower can perform. No longer an eyesore . . . it has personality and an aesthetic of movement." Both art and engineering, the design would make visible in its very materiality some of the haunted, uncanny qualities of the network often associated with cell towers. But in a beautiful form. People might even want something like this in their proverbial backyard, or neighborhood, or public square.

Aesthetics aside, Skylar Tibbits's design is fundamentally structural—in fact we might say it's infrastructural. In the computer or on paper, his tower resembles a 3D wireframe for some more finished object. The design is agnostic when it comes to the actual telecom equipment. Where would antennas be attached? At the top of the morphing towers? They aren't shown in the visualizations, but since his tower is made of cable-like tubes, I suppose that antennas and fiber-optics could conceivably be pulled through them and incorporated into the textile-like structure itself. This is a design fiction, a prototype to think with rather than an actual model to execute. It's also an example of materials prototyping. Tibbits is clearly interested in bringing to the surface the underlying properties and behaviors of the materials. He treats cell tower infrastructure as a design problem in its own right.

In this way Tibbits's tower recalls aspects of Italian Futurism, an early twentieth-century movement glorifying machinery and materials, celebrating the mechanical, electrical, artificial, and engineered objects of modernity. (Futurists such as Filippo Marinetti, for example, also reveled in violence and war and Futurism had close ties to Italian Fascism.) Milan architect Antonio Sant'Elia published a Futurist Manifesto in 1914 that proclaimed in its first two points:

1. That Futurist architecture is the architecture of calculation, of audacious temerity and of simplicity; the architecture of reinforced concrete, of steel, glass, cardboard, textile fiber, and of all those substitutes for wood, stone and brick that enable us to obtain maximum elasticity and lightness;

2. That Futurist architecture is not because of this an arid combination of practicality and usefulness, but remains art, i.e. synthesis and expression[.][15]

Key terms in point 1 (textile fiber, maximum elasticity, and lightness) could describe what's most important about the MIT cell tower. The morphing-mesh of the tower also owes something to a late twentieth-century style called blobitecture (from blob-architecture), identified with the work of Greg Lynn and Frank Gehry in particular.[16] Like objects designed in the Self-Assembly Lab, and ultimately in the spirit of calculation celebrated in the *Manifesto of Futurist Architecture*, blob-buildings and blobjects are highly dependent on computers and software to produce their complex biomorphic shapes. All of these approaches have in common an interest in the design of infrastructure itself, a kind of materials engineering *as* design. To think of cell towers as designable, in a way that would foreground their materials as well as their essential functions, might be one way to begin to come to grips with their increasing role in our everyday lives. It might help us to get a better sense of how much our handheld devices really require in the way of supporting infrastructure, to better understand how much their magic costs.

Tall towers in the background may eventually be replaced with many small antenna-boxes everywhere, if true 5G systems succeed the current 4G LTE standard.[17] In a kind of circular logic, the push for the Internet of Things and augmented reality (AR) is driving the development of the small-cell systems, whose initiatives require a dense mesh of antennas, sensors, and beacons that link together networks and objects such as autonomous vehicles and so-called smart appliances, mostly using the ultra-high frequencies of the RF spectrum. But a combination of big towers and small-cell systems is likely to persist for the foreseeable future. Giant towers, something like Skylar Tibbits's design (or other, different designs), may someday actually be deployed, but they will likely be just one part of the communications infrastructure. The question of who will design future cell towers, or whatever access-point objects eventually replace cell towers, remains open, along with the question of whether the towers will have designs on us.

6 COVERAGE

What does coverage mean when it comes to the cellular network? It's an ideal, an advertising claim, whether nationwide or global, something presumably mappable, roughly correlated with the number of cell towers a carrier has out there in the world. In 2013, artist Nickolay Lamm used his computer to create graphical images of what it might look like if all the cellular signals emanating from all the cell towers in Chicago and New York were visible.[1] His ingenious device was to shift the electromagnetic spectrum, to represent radio signals as if they were visible light. Each artwork shows a 3D cityscape with rainbow-colored translucent pyramids rising above a grid of hexagonal cells—the faint lines of which you can see if you look closely, floating just above and parallel to the streets and sidewalks, beneath the tops of buildings. In the Chicago image, one tower beams out radio frequency (RF) radiation, like light from a lighthouse, over the vast darkness of Lake Michigan. The overall result is lovely, but also vaguely claustrophobic, as if the artist Christo had draped the entire city in a gigantic sheet of brightly colored bubblewrap. Each peak of each pyramid of light represents a cell tower—or, since this is a depiction of a crowded downtown, usually a multidirectional antenna array mounted on a rooftop or a water tower. There are no visible gaps. Out at its far edges, the picture mimics the experience of flying in or out of Chicago's O'Hare International Airport at night and seeing the apparently infinite illuminated grid receding to the western horizon, as if the Earth were "lit from within / Like a poorly assembled electrical ball."[2]

Lamm's work is an interesting thought experiment in depicting the invisible. For one thing, it makes it easier to understand the telecom engineer's use of the word "shadow." What if some of that "light" were blocked by an obstacle? In a dense cityscape like Chicago's or New York's, some buildings do block cell signals, casting radio shadows. For another thing, Lamm's images effectively illustrate the 3D relationship of towers to the cellular grid. Each peak is placed at a corner of one of the hexagon-junctures, just as a tower would be in the cellular system, its antennas radiating in three directions. His graphs don't try to represent the countless tiny, ant-sized cellphones that would be swarming along at street level (and inside the multistoried buildings), each of which would have to connect, disconnect, and reconnect to a series of towers, one at a time, while moving around in the grid, in order to maintain coverage.

In practical terms, having coverage just means you get a signal when you want one. We experience it through an interface metaphor, the number of little bars on that received signal strength indicator (RSSI) icon on our screens. Even if we know that's not a precise measure, many of us till confuse the ideal of coverage with the reality of service. Telecom engineers differentiate between *coverage area* and *service area*. They recognize that there are white spots or dead zones in any coverage map, and gaps in the actual distribution of towers. Lamm's artworks remind us that the cellular grid itself is an abstraction: it hovers above the streets, an immaterial construct, an ideal geometry superimposed on the real conditions on the ground.[3] In practice, if you could see it, a combined service area like an inner city would look more like camouflage fabric, with a mosaic of biomorphic blobs, rather than the platonic ideal of Lamm's chickenwire or hex-block honeycomb. In his book on infrastructure, Brian Hayes says that "a map of cell boundaries is still recognizable as a honeycomb, even if it's one made by slightly drunken bees."[4] But if you're one of the ants (or bees) down in the grid, the tipsy irregularities matter when you're trying to connect.

Lamm's picture of New York City situates the viewer midtown, just above the rooftops, looking north toward Central Park, with the Hudson River and New Jersey in the distance to the left and Harlem straight ahead, past the park. As it turns out, this is almost exactly above the spot down on Sixth Avenue where the first handheld cellphone call was made on April 3, 1973.[5] You've probably heard this story before. Martin Cooper of Motorola was headed to a press conference at the Hilton when he stopped to use a prototype phone, the DynaTAC. It weighed 2½ pounds and looked like an oversized Lego prop, complete with a raised number-pad and two skeuomorphic red buttons with icons showing a handset "on the hook" or "off the hook." People would later refer to this as a Gordon Gekko phone, after the Michael Douglas character who used a commercial version in the 1987 movie, *Wall Street*. Cooper phoned a competitor at AT&T that day for a bit of friendly ribbing: "I'm calling you from a cellular phone, a real cellular phone, a handheld, portable, real cellular phone," he said, repeating the key term, "cellular," three times. Real cellphones wouldn't become widely available on the commercial market for another decade.

That origin story gets retold all the time, complete with the funny oversized prototype, and Cooper has posed for photographs on the spot to recreate the moment (in one later picture you can see people using phone booths right behind him). But very few versions of the story include the ur-cell site that he connected to. This was in a six-foot metal box on the roof of the fifty-story Burlington Consolidated Tower building a block uptown.[6] The base station was there to receive and send signals, to tie that unique first wireless handheld phone into the landline system. The press release from Motorola touted the new phone's ability to provide "communications in areas where conventional telephones are unavailable."[7] To do that, it needed towers.

That press release also referred to the DynaTAC as a "portable radio telephone." There had been radios in the trenches of battlefields, and heavy car phones with wired handsets and equipment under the seat or in the trunk, for decades. There were radio-based car phones by the 1940s. A basic cell system for mobile phones was invented as a concept back then, but it wasn't actually built—the necessary spectrum bandwidth wouldn't be available for decades. Historically, mobile assumed automobile, and the system of hexagonal cells and tower-to-tower handoffs was first implemented in the 1970s with moving automobiles in mind, as illustrated in a 1978 promotional film from AT&T showing little brightly colored cartoon cars driving across the grid from cell to cell and connecting to a succession of towers ("a high capacity system that will offer service to thousands of customers").[8] In the early 1990s my wife bought a used car that came with a phone. The handset was wired to a boxy transceiver under the rear seat and a special antenna was required. While she was driving around Chicago, her calls dropped sometimes, but the signal was usually pretty strong. New York was the first city slated for installation of the handheld system that Cooper demonstrated, and the goal was limited. The system was to allow you "to make telephone calls while riding in a taxi, walking down the city's streets, sitting in a restaurant or anywhere else a radio signal can reach."[9] Note the implicit acknowledgment that there would be places the radio signal would not reach, places without coverage.

I lived in New York City again in 2014–15, in an apartment just a few blocks from that midtown spot where Cooper made his demonstration call, close to the vantage point of Lamm's visualization. There were still places in Manhattan where my signal dropped—in the subway on the F-train, or down near Wall Street, or inside certain tall buildings, depending on the materials used in their construction. Everybody has experienced these "white spots" or "dead zones" in cities, shadows in hertzian space. Away from cities, there are even more significant gaps in coverage. Reliable coverage isn't evenly distributed—it's rarely even clearly defined. The coming 5G standard, with its new kinds of infrastructure, small cells with small antennas rather than traditional towers, may redraw the curve, but this will vary internationally and will probably still favor (maybe more than ever) urban and suburban areas over rural ones.

True 5G service is still in the future, as I write. To get a sense of the current limits of cellular coverage, I drove to Green Bank, West Virginia, where there are no cell towers. They're not allowed. On the day I left from the farm owned by family members, the gravel road had just washed out. Hurricane Michael had produced torrential rains and the creek had overwhelmed the culvert, so I coasted very slowly through deep water, engine idling, until I got to the paved road. Which got me thinking about infrastructure.

On my four-hour drive I passed over the Blue Ridge Parkway, through national forests, and through tunnels cut through mountains. This was coal country, but I saw a few signs reading "No Frack!" and "No Pipeline!" reminding me of the fraught history of Appalachia when it comes to utilities. The Tennessee Valley Authority (TVA) of the Works Progress Administration (WPA) brought rural electrification to the neglected area in the 1930s, stringing new lines on rows of giant pylons through the mountains to carry power from new hydroelectric dams. The WPA was created in 1935, just after the Federal Communications Commission (FCC) was founded (1934). The FCC aimed to make wired and wireless communications available to everyone in the country. The TVA and FCC targeted Appalachia and parts of the South where infrastructure was underdeveloped, an area with a culture of well-earned skepticism about the intentions of government agencies, private utilities, logging, mining, or pharmaceutical companies. Driving through Cass, West Virginia, a company town built in 1900 for the West Virginia Pulp and Paper Company, I saw streets of restored workers' whitewashed frame houses. At the main crossing an antique steam train waited to take tourists up the mountain. The railway originally carried lumber to a sawmill up the Greenbrier River.

I drove through many spots with no cell signal at all, especially down in the deep shadows (blocking both light and radio waves) created by the mountain hollows. As I approached the town of Green Bank, in Pocahontas County, all the bars on my iPhone faded away, leaving only a row of faint connection ghosts. Population 143, the town is famous for being cell-tower free—zero coverage, on purpose—which I thought about as I drove past a pole-mounted payphone in a parking lot at the edge of town. Green Bank is in the middle of the 13,000 square-mile National Radio Quiet Zone (NRQZ) created by an act of congress in 1958. It also lies within the smaller overlapping West Virginia Radio Astronomy Zone, with a ten-mile radius around the Green Bank Observatory. In that radius, no cell towers, no radio signals of any kind are permitted, not even a Wi-Fi router or wireless printer. Observatory employees cruise the streets with equipment scanning for violations. Radio silence is needed in order to operate the big telescope, one of the world's largest steerable models, with its white steel-mesh dish and protruding arm 485 by 328 feet across, a tilted parabola seen above the treetops from anywhere in town. Just as you need darkness in order to see the light of distant stars, you need radio silence (or as close as you can get to it) in order to hear faint signals from distant galaxies.

Speaking of space, I had been listening to map directions based on satellite data (as well as Wi-Fi and cellular signals) on my drive north. Once I entered the NRQZ, Siri fell silent and the map stopped responding, but I didn't need it to locate the Green Bank Telescope. I just looked up and there it was, its white dish set against the green mountains and blue sky. At the observation deck out in the field, a group of school kids were posing for selfies with the big telescope, even though they knew they wouldn't be able to upload the pictures until later, after their bus left the zone. Over in the research center, I ran into a scientist in the hallway and asked him what he thought about all the press about the NRQZ and he said tersely, "that's extraneous to what we do here," meaning physics and astronomy. We talked for a few minutes anyway about all those stories treating Green Bank as a weird throwback: local high schoolers live without texting and somehow survive! People still use phone booths! Journalism about the town's "1950s lifestyle" emphasizes the strangeness of choosing to live in a white spot on the map, where you have to sign a form stating you won't have Wi-Fi, a microwave, or a remote-control garage-door opener. The stories usually play up the benefits of face-to-face social encounters in a small rural community.[10] But on the whole I think they exaggerate the neo-Luddism of the locals. When I stopped at the public library, the big telescope was visible across the field at the back. Inside, there were several internet-connected workstations. Broadband cable and ethernet connections aren't banned, just Wi-Fi. People video chat or message one another on the internet as much as they like, just so long as nothing travels wirelessly. Only the airwaves are restricted.

Some people believe that radio frequency waves make them sick, and some of them have moved to Green Bank because they see it as a kind of town-sized Faraday cage. They don't believe the consensus of scientific studies showing no evidence their conditions are caused by the non-ionizing RF radiation. Some blame conspiracies for hiding the truth. A few live in log cabins with no electricity and avoid fluorescent lighting in public buildings. One RF-sensitive newcomer had an allergic skin reaction while addressing a meeting of the ham radio operators club and felt vindicated when an audience member confessed that he had a concealed cellphone in his pocket.[11] This kind of story can be used to exaggerate the number of such people in Green Bank, but it does say something about what the town is seen as a refuge *from,* aside from RF radiation: anxiety, alienation, isolation, loss of community, and living too fast and out of touch with nature, modernity itself. Having cellular coverage not only allows people to make calls, it takes them to the internet, where social media nastiness and commercial and political manipulation based on the exploitation of personal data dominate many user experiences. No wonder many welcome a space apart, a place with no coverage.

Not everyone feels this way. Some local residents choose to drive regularly to the town of Marlinton almost 30 miles to the south, where a cell tower at the edge of the zone is allowed to stand because it's aimed away from the Green Bank Telescope. They park or stand around the base of the tower, get a signal, make some calls, send a few texts, or go online for a bit. Green Bank residents come there in such numbers that a no-loitering sign has been posted.[12] Another cell signal excursion out of Green Bank takes you up to the Snowshoe Mountain Ski Resort, thirty minutes away. I decided to visit. At the end of a series of sharp switchbacks at the top of the mountain, I found the ski village quiet out of season, no snow, the lift grounded, very few people around, a lone woman riding the zipline above the main street while her companion stood below and took a cellphone video— which he was going to be able to upload on the spot. The Green Bank radio telescope might have been visible from a lift chair, had the lift been running, and assuming the mountain ridge didn't conceal it. I got a coffee at Starbucks and found the usual Wi-Fi connection there. Then I wandered back down the street until I spotted a micro-antenna hung on the façade of a clothing and equipment shop, a small box about the size and shape of the Wi-Fi routers attached to the ceilings in my university's classrooms. Sure enough, I had a few bars.

I had driven up to the resort to experience the fuzzy edge of supposedly ubiquitous coverage. On top of the mountain, flipping the usual metaphor, AT&T has created an oasis of connectivity, a small place with coverage in the midst of the NRQZ.[13] The antennas I saw were part of a distributed antenna system (DAS) that covers the ski resort with an array of those small boxes—a harbinger of 5G systems to come. The system is relatively weak, and it automatically reduces the power emitted by any cellphone that connects to it, creating what's referred to as a whisper network. Still, this seems to many like an oasis in the no-cell desert, one that many are eager to visit, even while extolling the benefits of the no-cell zone below. This seems like a parable of our collective ambivalence when it comes to the global coverage we say we want but still worry about having.

One dark corollary of total coverage is the possibility of total surveillance. On the western side of the NRQZ, in Pendleton County, is the perhaps more pressing reason for the zone's quiet: the National Security Administration's (NSA's) listening station near Sugar Grove.[14] (I didn't bother trying to visit this site.) It was established in 1959 around another giant radio telescope, this one built by the National Naval Research Laboratory. The location has been under the control of the NSA for most of its existence, exclusively so since the naval base closed in 2015. The mountaintop site, code-named Timberline, includes an underground bunker beneath its array of white dish antennas. Its surveillance activity includes monitoring satellite and cellular communications, both foreign and—after 9/11—domestic, as mentioned in materials released in 2013 by Edward Snowden. It's a strange paradox: the National Radio Quiet Zone was designed first to block, and later to listen in on, the nonstop communications afforded by the increasingly ubiquitous coverage surrounding it.

The advent of cell phones and cell towers complicated surveillance for law enforcement, as shown even in fictional representations over time. In the 1974 film, *The Conversation*, Gene Hackman plays an old-school surveillance specialist who intercepts suspects' calls using physical microphones, bugs, and tape decks. He only uses public phone booths, himself, and he refuses to own a phone. In the final scene he violently wrecks his own apartment looking for a suspected listening device. The award-winning TV series, *The Wire* (2002–8), juxtaposed street life with police work in Baltimore, including eavesdropping on drug dealers and gang members. In Season 3, a key plot thread involves the dealers' use of disposable candy-bar-shaped burner phones. The term burner has now been extended to refer to anonymous social media accounts, but it was new enough at the time that a character has to pause to explain it. Burner phones litter the streets, and people pick them up to see if they still have any minutes left on them. The police have trouble getting wiretap authorization before a batch of burners is discarded. "How are we supposed to put a wire on *that*?" one cop asks. At one point they use a Triggerfish cell-site simulator, a version of the Stingray, a suitcase-sized cell frequency identification device (CFID) that tricks suspects' phones into connecting with it instead of the nearest tower.[15] This allows them to intercept calls and record phone numbers. One character explains that "with the old analog machines you used to have to follow the guy around," but "with digital . . . you just pull the number right off the cell tower." Real-life law enforcement may sometimes still intercept cellphones in this way, or by getting a warrant for location data, but most everyday phone surveillance has relied on the call-record metadata collected by the telecom, the limitations of which are still poorly understood by the general public. David Simon, the creator of *The Wire*, said that the introduction of cellular technology "left police investigations vulnerable," so the show was sometimes asked to withhold details of new, unproven surveillance techniques that were being tested in real life.[16]

A 2014 podcast about a real crime in Baltimore, *Serial,* examined the 1999 murder of high school student, Hae Min Lee. Her ex-boyfriend Adnan Syed was indicted, based in part on his cellphone records, the list of calls tied to specific cell towers, evidence that was later called into question. This was the first case to rely on cellphone data of this kind. In 2016 a judge vacated the conviction and authorized a new trial, in part because Syed's lawyer hadn't properly questioned the cellular evidence.[17] As I write, an appeals court has ruled that Syed will not get a new trial because the issue of the evidence wasn't raised early enough, but he plans to appeal to the Supreme Court.[18] A follow-on podcast, *Undisclosed*, reinvestigated all the evidence and exposed its ambiguities. Syed's cellphone had supposedly pinged towers in the area of the wooded Leakin Park where the victim's body was found, according to AT&T call logs. But those logs are not objective evidence of location. A cover sheet attached to the phone records even included a disclaimer: "incoming calls will NOT be considered reliable for location information."[19] Official cellular coverage maps were entered into evidence during the trial, but their uncertainty was the basis of the requested retrial, as it emerged that mundane obstructions, such as dense foliage or a grassy hill, or a heavy call load at a given moment, could have determined which tower, or sector of a tower, Syed's phone was able to ping. And if two towers' coverage areas overlapped (as they sometimes do), either one might have been pinged from the same location. So-called drive testing in the field—using special equipment to see which towers are pinged—was also ruled inconclusive, since the events in question were in the past and conditions for interference might have changed. The notion that the authorities could determine Syed's precise location by looking at his call records was in the end refuted. In another case, a 2012 ruling blocked testimony about cellular location based on call records, "because the analyses did not rise to the level of trusted, replicable science."[20]

Hae Min Lee was murdered in 1999, before smartphones, when cellphones were still relatively new. Adnan Syed was one of the few in his circle to even own a cellphone and many of his fellow students still carried pagers.[21] One piece of evidence turned on a call made from a phone booth in the Best Buy parking lot. There was no such phone booth by the time the producers began making the *Serial* podcast. Possibly it was removed, like many others in that era.[22] But in the 2019 HBO TV special revisiting the case, one long shot of the Best Buy clearly shows a cell tower looming up behind the store, a graphic reminder of the mixed and changing infrastructure environment in which location and communication and coverage were (and still are) being defined.

Using call records, as the prosecutor did in that 1999 case, is different from the more recent practice of using GPS-generated location data, as tracked by Google's Location History. Law enforcement investigators can now do that too, getting so-called geofence warrants to scoop up location data from a suspect's phone (as well as adjacent others caught in the virtual dragnet).[23] A 2019 podcast, *To Live and Die in LA*, illustrates the difference. Its investigation of another murder demonstrated the more precise geolocation tracking that Google's technology now makes possible, compared with the making of *Serial* almost twenty years ago.[24] We wish for ever-more ubiquitous coverage while (rightly) fearing the surveillance that it makes possible. The good news may be that we haven't got our wish just yet. Cellular coverage is still in many cases an amorphous, unevenly distributed, contingent thing, taking place on the ground as much as in the air. Our devices rely on a mix of overlapping networks for calls, internet, location. The source of our data or signals isn't always clear in the moment. Part of the disoriented feeling we have in relation to the networks is the result of this kind of overlap, a designed feature of the cellular system and its methods for exploiting the spectrum.

In April 2018, artist Doug Aitken mounted an exhibit in New York City called *New Era,* about the global impact of cellular technology.[25] The space was designed with mirrors and multiple screens around the viewer to create a kaleidoscope of layered images, starting with that first Motorola DynaTAC, and including close-ups of circuit boards, towers, a radio antenna, all juxtaposed with images of the natural environment: shorelines, mountains, caves. The centerpiece was a brief video interview with the inventor, Martin Cooper himself. Sitting against a darkened background, he introduces himself and says that he and his team created the first cellular telephone. The ambient soundtrack swells and the images multiply. Suddenly we cut to Cooper in a close-up: "I made a phone call," he says quietly, and the phrase gets repeated and mixed with a techno beat, then stops. We see Cooper silhouetted from behind, on a beach: "Uh, and it's just not going to stop," he predicts.

The implication is that cellular technology is spreading in the way biological cells do, through exponential mitosis, to colonize the globe. In one sense this is plausible—there are now untold millions of cell towers around the world, and with the trend toward the microcells in 5G networks, there may soon be uncountable small antennas embedded in many places. But not everywhere all at once, not evenly, and not without resistance from the stubborn materialities of infrastructure itself and of the global environment. These constraints continue to cast shadows over the imagined grid of hexagonal cells—an abstraction that preceded and still guides the construction of the infrastructure that supports our collective dream of seamless, ubiquitous coverage.

7 ON EARTH

In this book, the cell tower has been the object of attention. But from the perspective of global communications, the whole point is to have a lot of them, spread out in the world. The cell tower is an object worth seeing in its own right, but it's also part of a much larger and harder to see object—in the way a single bird can be part of a massive, undulating flock—the multitude of cell towers on Earth. The traditional steel cell tower may be replaced over time by many small-cell antennas, at least in some places. It's even possible that device-to-device technologies (D2D) will be added to the mix, with any two phones that are close enough to one another being able to communicate directly, walkie-talkie style.[1] But these changes would only amount to a kind of fractal multiplication of the "towers" (or access points, in whatever form) within the vast terrestrial network. "All-the-cell-towers" on Earth is a hard thing to wrap your head around. To begin with, it's just hard to count them all. There's no reliable estimate of the total number—certainly there are many millions. But how do we take into account all the small-cell antennas that already exist, and the multiple carriers served by a single tower (co-location)? What about the different tallies of cell sites made by carriers and governments around the world?

To begin to think about all-the-cell-towers we have to imagine it/them as part of the varied global environment, installed one tower at a time on deforested mountainsides, along highways, beside algae-blooming shores, on tall rooftops, sticking up amid trees, antennas and other components requiring regular maintenance—sometimes by workers climbing them—and yet also humming away in the night when no one's looking. All-the-cell-towers is the kind of large-scale thing that philosopher Michel Serres calls a "world-object."[2] That is, an object with at least one dimension that corresponds to a dimension of the world itself, such as space or time. World-objects include the satellite, the atom bomb, the internet, nuclear waste, and the mobile telephone system. Are global communications networks world-objects? Serres asks (rhetorically). "They have neither the presence nor probably the reality of objects since channels and fibre optics transport numbers, symbols and virtualities." But their scale is global: they collapse space. We don't just interact with them, he says, "[w]e inhabit them instead."[3] For Serres, "World-objects put us in the presence of a world that we can no longer treat as an object . . . it acts, in turn, on the global constraints of our survival."[4]

Serres may overemphasize the virtual when it comes to the world-object of digital communications.[5] Timothy Morton's similar concept, hyperobjects, agnostically considers the weird existence of all kinds of large-scale objects, whether digital or not, whether made by humans or not, all "massively distributed in time and space relative to humans"[6]—a black hole, all the nuclear material on Earth, a massive oil field, global warming, the Florida Everglades. Hyperobjects "are not just collections, systems, or assemblages of other objects. They are objects in their own right."[7] They are pervasive and "non-local" in their effects. As Serres said in reference to global communications, we inhabit hyperobjects, we live inside *them*, uncertainly oriented in relation to their vast dimensions. And yet their footprints, their local manifestations, impress our everyday lives, in the way that weather impinges upon us as a manifestation of global warming. At one point Morton borrows an image from Martin Heidegger to picture hyperobjects "towering-through . . . into the misty transcendentalism of modernity."[8] All-the-cell-towers, the multitude distributed out in the world, towers-through into the misty conceptual vagueness of our assumptions regarding the network and its invisibility, ethereality, and ubiquity. It looms in our peripheral vision, at the edge of our awareness. We know all those towers are there, but the handoffs keep taking place as we move around. We're never sure which tower we're pinging. It's like trying to trace a massive undulating flock of birds. From the inside. Or, better yet, like trying to trace all the flocks around the world at a given moment, not knowing whether you're inside or outside them.

Here's an image: a flock of screeching birds swirls like a dark tornado around a steel-lattice cell tower set against the backdrop of a cloudy sunrise. A man approaches with his arms raised, then opens the security fence and hangs himself from the tower—within the tower—at the center of the whirlwind of flapping wings. This is from the opening credits of the 2018 Tamil-language Indian science-fiction movie, *2.0*. Not long into the story, we see millions of cellphones squirting out of people's hands, the first after a motorcyclist gets a mysterious incoming call with a chirping bird video on the screen. All the cellphones fly up and away, agglomerating into a series of shape-shifting forms, eventually morphing into a colossal bird of prey with shining red eyes, its feathers made up of thousands of shiny, clacking cellphones. Its first act is to rip up the cell tower we saw in the opening scene by its concrete roots. Soon all the cell towers in the area are being destroyed.

The big bird is a kind of Kaiju, a monster from the genre of Japanese film that includes Godzilla, Mothra, and Hedorah (a.k.a. the Smog Monster, who rises from the toxic swamp but morphs into a flying form). In keeping with the conventions, the giant cellphone bird destroys buildings and flips over cars and swoops down to kill people as they run screaming down the street. Glass high-rise façades are shattered, there are fiery explosions, and the military gets involved. Revenge is the motive, as is often the case in movies of this kind, the attacks coming as payback for earlier injustice, whether the atom bomb or a chemical disaster. In this case the antagonist is a mystical ornithologist who runs a bird sanctuary, enraged over the mass killing of birds by cell-tower radiation.

He's the one we saw hanging himself from a cell tower in the film's opening, after his protests against telecoms failed, and he gets transformed into a bird-man controlling the giant cellphone monster. The big bird is a transparent metaphor for our collective anxieties about cellphones and cell towers, associated with broader anxieties about ecological disaster, including impending mass extinctions. *2.0* starts with a vague disclaimer that the film is "based on articles which have appeared in various newspapers and social media platforms" (the words appear over blurry images of the newspaper articles and headlines); it's only a work of fiction, no resemblance to anyone living or dead, etc. Building on tabloid stories and pseudoscience, it draws on real anxieties, whatever their basis, and, in its over-the-top way, the movie calls attention to the volatility of the global environment and (inadvertently) the surprising fragility of the cellular network itself in the face of that volatility.

What are the facts? An estimated 6.6 million birds, especially night-migrating birds, die every year through direct collisions with broadcast towers and cell towers.[9] Guy-wired towers pose the greatest hazard, since the birds can crash into the wires as well as the towers. These are collisions with physical obstructions, and this problem isn't unique to cell towers: birds also crash into glass skyscrapers and wind-turbines. These are real ecological concerns that deserve attention. But the movie blames invisible electromagnetic radiation, not collisions with towers. Scientific studies have shown no clear link between the invisible radio frequency

(RF) emissions of cell towers and the health of birds or other animals, including humans. Some studies *have* suggested, theoretically, that electromagnetic "noise" in the environment might affect birds' ability to navigate, but none has explicitly tested the RF radiation of cell towers.[10] The premise of *2.0* loosely extrapolates from the scientific theory of the radical-pair mechanism, in which molecular-scale proteins in birds' eyes serve as tiny compasses, orienting them in relation to the Earth's electromagnetic field.[11] Given this mechanism, the speculation goes, a navigating songbird might conceivably fly too close to a cell tower at night, experience radio static that interferes with its magneto-navigation, and crash into the tower or fall to Earth. The film's undulating flock of cellphones represents the amorphous object, all-the-cellphones. (Commentary accompanying the streaming film reveals that over one million actual smartphones were used in making the clacking special effects!) "Technology surrounds us, but we are misusing technology," the hero intones at the end. We should "coexist, control radiation, reduce networks. The Earth doesn't belong only to us." And yet, the movie ends with a Bollywood-style dance number celebrating two cyborgs in love. After all, an army of tiny robots *have* just saved the day, in cooperation with a massive flock of real white doves.

The pseudoscientific entertainment calls attention to a larger truth: cell towers are earthly objects. They are in the world, act on the world, and on us—even if not in the ways the film imagines—and they are in turn vulnerable to the world's actants and accidents. To actually build cellular infrastructure, engineers have to engage the particulars of the physical environment. All-the-cell-towers, a very large-scale hyperobject that we can barely imagine, is vulnerable in the face of the even larger, enveloping, hyperobject of global warming and its effects.

To drive to the Florida Keys, I take the Tamiami Trail (Highway 41) out of Naples across the heart of the Everglades. It's mostly a long, straight, vanishing-point road. Soon I leave behind the strip malls and housing developments for lots of sandy palmetto scrub and, later, glimpses of saw grass, with occasional hardwood hammocks (clusters of trees). Along the side of road, there are chain-link fences for much of the way, with trees held behind them, sometimes a marshy ditch with a slow-wading egret or blue heron, and I know there are plenty of snakes and alligators, though I don't see them on every trip. The Everglades National Park remains contested ground after many years of displacement, reengineering, pollution, and habitat destruction. It's an impressive 1.5 million acres, which, even after many traversals and using a map on a cellphone propped in the cupholder, still feels *indeterminately* big. The size—or precise geological epoch—of the Everglades is hard to get a handle on. It's a hyperobject in its own right, as Timothy Morton says. Fresh water from Lake Okeechobee flows south—at least nominally, where it still can, given generations of human intervention, development, phosphate mining, agriculture (especially by the sugar industry), dikes and canals, followed by some limited efforts at restoration in recent years. As I write, the new governor of Florida is preparing to allow oil drilling in the park.

The rare cell tower at the edge of the Everglades is visible for many miles across the grassy expanse. But occasionally a dead cypress or a lone palm catches my eye and for a minute I'm confused. About midway in my trip across the state, my bars drop to zero. I see circling raptors: buzzards, red-shouldered hawks, and ospreys, also known as fish hawks, which were endangered in my childhood from DDT and other pesticides but are now coming back (as they say) across Florida and elsewhere. Ospreys are dark, with a white breast and neck and a six-foot wingspan. They build four- to five-foot nests as high as possible, where they can have a clear 360-degree view. Radio transmission towers, power-line pylons, and cell towers are among their preferred spots, along with boating navigation signs standing out in the water or cypress trunks protruding from the mangroves. On power lines and cell towers they can get electrocuted, or their nests can catch fire from shorted wires. So conservation organizations, utility companies, and telecoms build alternative roosts, some looking like wooden shipping pallets and some like fiberglass satellite TV dishes, bolted to the top of tall wooden posts. You can find plans online for building your own.[12] Some fake-tree cell towers come with ready-made nests built in, placed for optimal safety for both bird and tower. But the traditional triangular antenna array remains attractive to the birds, where they are protected behind panel antennas but have a wide-angle view.

Skirting the Greater Miami sprawl, I turn south on US Highway 1 to Homestead, then cross the Overseas Highway to the Florida Keys, where the sky opens up. On the northern end of Key Largo, I spot the weird cell site I'm looking for: a blocky concrete tower shaped like a toy periscope, with a shallow box protruding at the top (like a lens-opening), facing south, and a smaller one (like an eyepiece) lower down, facing north (Figure 10). Two rows of oblong-panel cellular antennas are bracketed around the top. The two boxes look like brutalist hotel balconies, and in fact I see two workers standing on the upper one. When I stop to take a closer look, they're using a block and tackle to lift a bundle to the top. An old basketball backboard without a rim is mounted at the base of the tower, a poignant remnant of more recreational times at the site.

This was formerly a Bell South microwave tower, constructed 1975–6. Local residents still call it that—the microwave tower—and they use it as a wayfinding landmark when they're out on the water. It went up after the heyday of the AT&T Long Lines or Skyway relay system, which began operation in 1951, a transcontinental network carrying television broadcasts as well as phone calls from tower to tower. The towers varied in design but tended to be either a square latticework structure, looking like construction-site scaffolding with large horn-shaped reflector antennas—sometimes called sugar-scoop antennas—or set on top of a city building, with the horn antennas integrated into the

FIGURE 10 Microwave tower in Key Largo, Florida. Author's photograph.

design. A good number were also concrete towers similar to the one on Key Largo. It was a cold war system designed to withstand a nuclear attack. Most of the Long Lines towers were sold by the end of the century,[13] but many still stand, graffiti-marked and crumbling.[14]

The Key Largo tower may have been peripherally connected to that system, providing a short link to the southern Keys. I'm not sure. But its original transmission system was clear. One striking polaroid photo from the year of its completion shows that it once had two huge, white microwave-drum antennas, set side by side in the top balcony, aimed slightly to one side (Figure 11).[15] With the upper balcony looking like a big square head above a gaping mouth, the round antennas resemble two blank eyes. (The photo doesn't show what's in the lower balcony, but probably there was a matching pair of drums there, facing the other way. Microwave antennas of this kind typically came in pairs: one for transmitting and one for receiving. Most likely the

FIGURE 11 Microwave tower with drum antennas, 1976, in Key Largo, Florida. Photo courtesy Monroe County Property Appraiser's Office, Monroe County, Florida.

site would have had two pairs.) A skinny antenna mast on top completes the effect. The tower looks like a giant space alien or robot—or a mecha-type monster in a Kaiju film—cutting its eyes sideways. (The graininess of the polaroid only adds to this cinematic impression.) It makes basic design sense that a system requiring line-of-sight connections from tower to tower might end up with something resembling a face with eyes. I don't know exactly when the big drums were removed, but around 2012, the by-then eyeless robot-alien was converted into a modern cell tower with the addition of the usual antennas and cables.[16]

The Key Largo site is just one of many weird towers across Florida, from the ornate Bok Tower in Lake Wales (with a working carillon), to bat towers for mosquito control in the Keys, to themed tourist attractions, like the Citrus Tower in Clermont, or the 240-foot Lake Placid Tower off Highway 27 (Figure 12). The Lake Placid Tower was built in 1960 from almost 100,000 concrete blocks and once claimed to be the tallest concrete-block structure in the world, for what it was worth.[17] It was built on the Lake Wales Ridge, a relatively high-elevation sandy spine (about 300 feet at the high point) down the middle of the flat state, the remnant of a string of islands from when the peninsula was under water millions of years ago. On the way into town, you pass orange groves, cows grazing under live oaks, fast food restaurants, and gas stations. The shuttered tower still dominates its now-defunct strip mall. It once had busy observation decks and a restaurant at the top, capped with

FIGURE 12 Lake Placid Tower in Lake Placid, Florida. Author's photograph.

big aluminum decorations, like a crazy crest. Now there's a blank marquee at the base. It was repurposed in 2003 as yet another ad hoc cell tower, by adding two tiers of panel antennas to the concrete exterior. The site always featured telephony. In its heyday, tourists were encouraged to visit the restaurant where they could "phone home on 'Florida's highest payphone.'"[18]

Concrete, whether as blocks or poured around rebar, is a common building material in Florida, because it stands up to both termites and hurricanes. The robot-alien tower on Key Largo was perhaps hardened not only against possible nuclear attack but against the tropical storms that threaten the state every summer. Many projections have the lower portion of the overpopulated and overdeveloped state of Florida entirely underwater by the next century. In that context, the Key Largo tower is a reminder of the limits of technology in the face of environmental forces. That's true not only in Florida, of course. Google "cell tower storm damage" and you'll see pages and pages of images of what the weather can do, probably including one tornado-twisted tower in Little Axe, Oklahoma, in May 2010, its steel lattice spiraled out of shape and tucked under like the neck of a heron, and in March 2019, a latticework tower brought down by a tornado across Route 280 in Alabama, cables tangled with pine-tree branches (real ones), panel antennas sticking up at crazy angles like broken teeth, brackets bent, and fiberglass covers ripped open, exposing small metal antennas inside.

In the aftermath of Hurricane Irma, in August–September 2017, portable towers on flatbed trucks were set up as usual to re-establish a precarious connectivity in the northern Keys. Called COWs (cells on wheels) or COLTs (cells on light trucks), these are typically deployed to boost connectivity or to provide connectivity where it has gone down, whether during an emergency like a natural disaster, or at an outdoor concert or other large public event. A trailer or truck is rolled in and the tower is raised on it, sometimes a pneumatic extendable monopole mast and sometimes a small lattice tower, sometimes with self-assembling guy-wires pre-attached to the trailer base or staked out on the ground. The cute-animal acronyms (COW and COLT) make these mobile base stations sound like livestock to be released into the field or wrangled into places they are needed. A COW was set up to provide temporary service in place of that tornado-felled tower on Alabama's Route 280, for example, and they were used following California wildfires, as well as after hurricanes in the Florida Keys.

The Keys' location on the edge of the continental US— Key West was once called the Gibraltar of the West—has

FIGURE 13 Wireless antenna with wooden towers in Key West, Florida. Photo, Florida Postcard Collection, ed. Laura Runge, University of South Florida.

made them an important site for wireless communications.[19] About 100 miles southwest of the Key Largo robot-alien tower, you can stand near the waterfront in old Key West, at the intersection of Caroline and Whitehead Streets, hear the seabirds and glimpse the water through the trees. On that spot in 1906 an equilateral triangle with 300-foot sides marked the base of a trio of wooden towers rising 200 feet above the rooftops, making up a wireless telegraph station (Figure 13). Each tower or pole was 3 feet wide at the base and tapered to about a foot at the top. They were made from big timbers bolted together and guy-wired with cables, then linked around their tops with a wire-mesh aerial—hundreds of pounds of phosphor bronze wire, like a metallic cloud floating above the conch-style houses and palm trees below. This was a Florida relative of Marconi's multi-tower aerial in Cornwall, built around the same time (1901). That Key West neighborhood was once part of a US naval base. The three towers formed a link in a long chain of wireless stations connecting the mainland US to the northern Keys, Key West, Cuba, Puerto Rico, and Panama. Marconi himself had demonstrated to the US navy the potential usefulness of such a wireless network. There were two related sites in Key West, the transmitter station to the west, down on Caroline Street, and a receiver station near the eastern shore of the island. In 1914, the bolted timber masts were moved out to the eastern site and three steel towers were erected downtown in their place, where they remained for sixty years. One photo on old postcards shows the 300-foot steel towers looming above

Whitehead Street, their tops linked with cables supporting antenna wire (Figure 14). The steel towers were in turn replaced in 1969 with a single microwave tower.

Another old photo shows the naval base as seen *from* one of the steel towers, looking down vertiginously from the perspective of the tower itself, or from the perspective of the camera held by whoever climbed up there (Figure 15). When I look at the photo, my eye is caught by the steel struts in the foreground, some slightly out of focus at the photographer's feet, like the one being held onto by a free hand, I have to assume. The camera's aperture captures something like the tower's own point of view, and I can't help but think of Walter

BIRD'S EYE VIEW, SHOWING U.S. NAVAL AND WIRELESS STATION, KEY WEST, FLA.

FIGURE 14 Wireless antenna with steel towers in Key West, Florida. Photo, Florida Postcard Collection, ed. Laura Runge, University of South Florida.

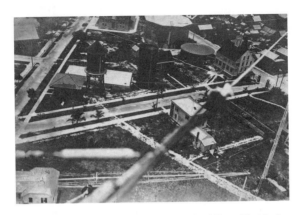

FIGURE 15 View of US naval base in Key West, Florida from a wireless tower. In Thomas Neil Knowles, "The US Navy Wireless Telegraph Stations at Key West and Dry Tortugas," *Florida Keys Sea Heritage Journal* 19.1 (Fall 2008), 1–16.

Benjamin's description of the Eiffel Tower as a "monument" to the "heroic age of technology,"[20] along with his quoted description of the view from the tower, or from another impressive set of latticework towers, the pylons of the giant Rochefort Transporter Bridge:

> In the windswept stairways of the Eiffel Tower, or, better still, in the steel supports of a Pont Transbordeur, one meets with the fundamental aesthetic experience of present-day architecture: through the thin net of iron that hangs suspended in the air, things stream—ships, ocean, houses, masts, landscape, harbor. They lose their

distinctive shape, swirl into one another as we climb downward, merge simultaneously.[21]

From the perspective of the tower, many things come in and out of focus. The cell tower was born in the late twentieth century, descended from earlier wireless towers. Now cell towers cover vast areas of the Earth and all-the-cell-towers forms an infrastructural "net" through which other "things stream." New cell towers are still being built, though with the sense, now, that the traditional ones may soon be replaced or supplemented, just as they replaced and supplemented earlier generations of radio, telegraph, and telephone towers. But not all of them, not all at once.

In February 2019, a company named Ubiquitilink sent a prototype satellite into low Earth orbit to function as a cell tower in space.[22] Their website calls for increasing global coverage to include the roughly 75 percent of the world currently still without cell service.[23] They plan to have 24–36 new satellites in low Earth orbit by 2021 and (however improbably) thousands of them by 2023, at which point "coverage will be continuous, whether in the middle of the Saharan Desert, the Amazon jungle, or the Pacific Ocean." The satellite system is designed on the economic model of today's cell tower system, with UbiquitiLink leasing space on the satellites to carriers to enable co-location and global roaming. Satellite phones already exist, of course. They've long been used by the military, journalists, and others in remote locations, war zones, or during natural disasters, where cell phone service is unavailable. In 1999, a number of contingency plans for responding to a possible worldwide Y2K computer systems failure included using satellite phones. But UbiquitiLink aims to turn any plain, unmodified cell phone into a satellite phone, using an app to connect to their constellation of orbiting towers (as it were), with the goal of replacing "inoperable terrestrial communications" in white spaces or during future disasters. The ambition is "to connect the phones in our pockets anywhere on the planet, all of the time."[24]

In one sense, of course, this is typical startup hype. But it also echoes familiar telecom rhetoric about providing universal, impervious coverage, the rhetoric in this case literally elevated, in the spirit of Gemini, Apollo, or SpaceX. (Elon Musk's SpaceX is launching its own Starlink constellation of satellites for providing worldwide broadband internet service.) It's true that a phone with an unobstructed line of transmission straight up to a satellite in low Earth orbit—under about 300 miles—is more likely to connect than it would be when trying to ping a terrestrial cell tower from down in a mountain hollow, or in the aftermath of a hurricane. And the company claims it has software fixes to manage problems like the doppler shift (and consequent lag) caused by the swiftly orbiting cell towers flying overhead. They say they've tested a basic 2G connection on their prototype satellite. The plan is to offer E-911 emergency texting as a free backup service (just as 911 dialing is available on current cellphones), but additional charges will likely be expensive, even though the signal to and from space may not be strong enough at first for large data transfers or even voice calls. Another concern is that this system would concentrate universal orbital connectivity in the hands of a single company (we've seen how that usually works out). Moreover, low orbit is still *of* the Earth if not technically on it. Maintenance of a constellation of thousands of satellites, including syncing their clocks and updating their software, will require massive terrestrial infrastructure, just as today's GPS systems do. If this ambitious plan were to work, a satellite cell tower system would likely supplement rather than replace the older steel towers and the coming 5G small-cells, at least for the foreseeable future.

There's another potential danger. A future cellular system flying too high to see with the naked eye (under most conditions) might well be treated as even more invisible and ethereal—more easily unseen—than terrestrial cell towers have been. It would then become necessary to remind ourselves again to look up at the night sky to spot the sweeping dot of light, the cell tower in space, to see the orbital infrastructure, even if partly in our mind's eye, to remind ourselves that the fast-moving star is actually a relatively small metal, glass, silicon, and wire object launched into orbit through extraordinary means and at great expense. Whether installed on the surface of the Earth or in orbit around it, infrastructure is never seamless or impervious. Many of us are starting to understand this, as the hyperobject of global warming is busy revealing the extent to which all human-made objects are themselves vulnerable, precarious, never without costs.

When tropical storm Debby stalled in the Gulf of Mexico in June 2012, it spawned scattered tornadoes across Florida, including one that skipped down my alley and shook my house, blew out some windows, ripped off nearby roofs, and flooded the streets on our barrier island. Power went down, but somehow cell service stayed up. I was lucky. My most pressing communication problems for a few days were charging my phone's battery and finding Wi-Fi. Four months later, Hurricane Sandy slammed into the eastern seaboard, wreaking massive destruction, killing almost 300, and knocking out approximately 25 percent of all the cellphone connections in its path.[25] Many (so many) storms since then have disrupted cell service in places around the world (while causing much worse forms of suffering and destruction than mere loss of cellular service). These days, the flatbed COWs with humming generators and antennas that are brought in on such occasions have begun to look like normal, everyday communications. Infrastructure—without which there is no cellular network—is never truly invisible, ethereal, ubiquitous, or impervious. To begin to appreciate this, and to begin to better understand our dependence on the network, we need to learn to *see* the cell tower, whatever form it takes.

FIGURES

ACKNOWLEDGMENTS

My thanks to Haaris Naqvi, Chris Schaberg, Ian Bogost, and everyone at Bloomsbury for their support, and respect to Alice Marwick for the brilliant cover designs for this book and the series as a whole that first drew me in. Colleagues and friends helped in various ways: Laura Runge supported my research and, coincidentally, created the Florida Postcard Collection, which Lynette Kuliyeva searched for towers. John Lennon alerted me when new equipment was going in at a local site. Ryan Carney patiently answered a question about birds. Geoffrey Rockwell compared cellphone photos of the Telmex Torre de Comunicaciones over mescals one evening. I'm also grateful to the bartender at the Terry Bison Ranch, the technician who let me into the ground space, the scientist in the hallway of the Green Bank Observatory, the pastor in Tampa, and Terry Hinton and James Gale of the Monroe County Property Appraisers Office in the Keys. Finally, thank you and I'm sorry to everyone who tolerated my obsessive cellspotting during the writing of this book, including Rebecca, who always asked how it was going, and (as ever) Heidi, who gamely played along with my treating each tower as another weird and fascinating roadside attraction.

NOTES

Chapter 1

1 Walter Benjamin, *The Arcades Project*, trans. Howard Eiland and Kevin McLaughlin (Cambridge, Massachusetts, and London: Belknap Press of Harvard University Press, 1999), 887.

2 Eiffel Tower website, https://www.toureiffel.paris/en/the-monu ment/key-figures. (All internet sources were accessed June 2019.)

3 Eiffel Tower website, https://www.toureiffel.paris/en/the-monu ment/eiffel-tower-and-science.

4 Brian Hayes, *Infrastructure: A Field Guide to the Industrial Landscape* (New York and London: W. W. Norton & Co., 2005), 304.

5 Rob Walker, *The Art of Noticing* (New York: Penguin Random House, 2019), Kindle ed. Among the book's 131 game-like exercises is "spot something new every day," which comes with a list of potential mundane objects one might notice, including security cameras, payphones, stray traffic cones, and cellphone towers (loc. 216).

6 Your location is more likely to be divulged through GPS. See Jennifer Valentino-DeVries, "Google's Sensorvault Is a Boon for Law Enforcement. This is How it Works," *The New York Times*,

April 13, 2019, https://www.nytimes.com/2019/04/13/techn
ology/google-sensorvault-location-tracking.html.

7 Scientific studies have shown no link between the non-
ionizing radio waves of cellphones and health effects in
humans. And there's even less evidence for potential health
effects from the radiation you're exposed to from 100-foot
cell towers. See the summaries at the Australian Centre for
Electromagnetic Bioeffects Research website, https://acebr.uow.
edu.au/eme/index.html; and the World Health Organization's
"Electromagnetic Fields and Public Health: Mobile Phones,"
https://www.who.int/news-room/fact-sheets/detail/electr
omagnetic-fields-and-public-health-mobile-phones.

8 In the 2019 BBC Radio show, *New Ways of Seeing*, Episode 1,
"Invisible Networks," broadcast April 2019, https://www.bbc.co.uk/
programmes/m000458m, James Bridle spots microwave
antennas carrying data—including massive financial
transactions—across the urban rooftops of shuttered factories,
an emblem of how economic inequality is bound up with
everyday infrastructure: "If we can't see it, it's hard to think
about it." Writing about a different infrastructure arena,
Christopher Schaberg argues that, "[i]n order to contentiously
change them, in one way or another, we have to learn to see
airports, first," in *Airportness: The Nature of Flight* (London and
New York: Bloomsbury Academic, 2017), 88.

Chapter 2

1 Shannon Mattern, *Code and Clay, Data and Dirt: Five
Thousand Years of Urban Media* (Minneapolis: University of
Minnesota Press, 2017), 1.

2 Anthony Dunne, *Hertzian Tales: Electronic Products, Aesthetic Experience, and Critical Design* (Cambridge, Massachusetts: MIT Press, 2006), 101.

3 Shannon Mattern, *Code and Clay, Data and Dirt*, 1–2, discusses the Architecture of Radio app as one example of a recent trend: of making "'visible' the 'invisible' networks powering the wired world's digital economies, institutions, and lifestyles" (1).

4 Ibid., 1–3.

5 Ibid., 14.

6 Ibid., 5, 19, 31.

7 Ibid., 6. Mattern connects the modernism of the Eiffel Tower with later utilitarian infrastructure, including cell towers.

8 Ibid., 6.

9 Tesla Science Center website, https://teslasciencecenter.org/history/.

10 Jonathan Adolf Wilhelm Zenneck, *Wireless Telegraphy*, 151 (fig. 184). The apt comparison to Stonehenge is made by Brian Hayes in describing an array in Dixon, California, in *Infrastructure: A Field Guide to the Industrial Landscape* (New York and London: W. W Norton & Co., 2005), 302.

11 Vincze Miklós, "Photos from the Days When Thousands of Cables Crowded the Skies," *Gizmodo*, io9, September 3, 2014, https://io9.gizmodo.com/photos-from-the-days-when-thousands-of-cables-crowded-t-1629961917.

12 Biblioteca de México día con día website, "La Ciudadela y sus alrededores: Centro Telefónico San Juan," http://alrededoresciudadela.blogspot.com/2015/09/centro-telefonico-san-juan.html.

13 In the United States, bandwidth has historically been assigned by lottery and by auction. There are different possibilities for providing access to the spectrum, including conceiving of it as a commons to be managed rather than as property to be leased. See Jane C. Hu, "We're Running out of Spectrum for both Old and New Technologies," *SLATE*, May 29, 2019, https://slate.com/technology/2019/05/spectrum-auction-bandwidth-weather-forecasting-fcc-noaa.html, which points to a new concern: that coming 5G systems could infringe on the frequencies used by government agencies to predict and monitor the weather.

14 Lizzie Wade, "Where Cellular Networks Don't Exist, People are Building Their Own," *Wired*, January 14, 2015, https://www.wired.com/2015/01/diy-cellular-phone-networks-mexico/; Rhizomatica website, https://www.rhizomatica.org; Nina Lakhan, "'It Feels Like a Gift': Mobile Phone Co-op Transforms Rural Mexican Community," *The Guardian,* August 15, 2016, https://www.theguardian.com/world/2016/aug/15/mexico-mobile-phone-network-indigenous-community.

15 Rhizomatica website, https://www.rhizomatica.org.

16 Nina Lakhan, "'It Feels Like a Gift': Mobile Phone Co-op Transforms Rural Mexican Community," *The Guardian,* August 15, 2016, https://www.theguardian.com/world/2016/aug/15/mexico-mobile-phone-network-indigenous-community.

17 Adam Greenfield, *Radical Technologies: The Design of Everyday Life* (London: Verso, 2017), 13.

18 Ibid., 13.

19 Ibid., 13.

20 Ibid., 23.

Chapter 3

1 Fears of the potential dangers of 5G systems have been stoked by the RT America TV network in what looks like a familiar disinformation campaign, according to William J. Broad, "Your 5G Phone Won't Hurt You. But Russia Wants You to Think Otherwise," *The New York Times,* May 12, 2019, https://www.nytimes.com/2019/05/12/science/5g-phone-safety-health-russia.html.

2 Joyce Kilmer, "Trees" (*Poetry: A Magazine of Verse*, August 1913, 2:6, 160), Poetry Foundation, https://www.poetryfoundation.org/poetrymagazine/poems/12744/trees. A 1932 parody by Ogden Nash names a different infrastructural blight: "I think that I shall never see / A billboard lovely as a tree / Indeed, unless the billboards fall / I'll never see a tree at all" ("Song of the Open Road," *The New Yorker*, October 7, 1932, 18).

3 William Gibson, *Spook Country* (New York: Putnam's, 2007), 157–8.

4 Lisa Parks, "Around the Antenna Tree: The Politics of Infrastructural Visibility," *Flow* (March 6, 2009), https://www.flowjournal.org/2009/03/around-the-antenna-tree-the-politics-of-infrastructural-visibilitylisa-parks-uc-santa-barbara/.

5 Historically, military camouflage has also included "dazzle" patterns, which don't resemble anything in particular but disrupt and confuse perception.

6 Raycap | STEALTH engagements: https://www.stealthconcealment.com: "the fast-growing wireless industry depends on antennas. And STEALTH® has spent 25 years making them disappear."

7   Michael Chen and Justin Snider, "Signal Space," MKCA, http://mkca.com/projects/signal-space/. The Signal Space project is discussed in Shannon Mattern, *Code and Clay, Data and Dirt: Five Thousand Years of Urban Media* (Minneapolis: University of Minnesota Press, 2017), 34-36.

8   Christian Giggenbach, "The Greenbrier Wants Cell Tower to Look Like Pine Tree," *The Register-Herald*, Beckley, West Virginia, August 1, 2007, https://www.register-herald.com/news/local_news/the-greenbrier-wants-cell-tower-to-look-like-pine-tree/article_fd84787c-a280-54ea-a7b7-2f68b628314e.html.

9   Christian M. Giggenbach, "Greenbrier Pine Tree Cell Tower Helping Community," *The Register-Herald*, Beckley, West Virginia, September 28, 2008, https://www.register-herald.com/news/local_news/greenbrier-pine-tree-cell-tower-helping-community/article_e98fa465-c9ef-595e-8c27-d147f480baed.html.

10 "Ken Caryl, Colorado: Cellular Village," Roadside America, https://www.roadsideamerica.com/tip/8326.

11 Terry Bison Ranch website, https://www.terrybisonranch.com.

12 Congressional Resolution Designating November 7, 2015, as National Bison Day, from US Government Publishing Office, https://www.govinfo.gov/content/pkg/BILLS-114sres300ats/html/BILLS-114sres300ats.htm.

Chapter 4

1   Telecom Law Firm website, http://telecomlawfirm.com.

2   Michael Fisher (MrMobile), "How Cell Towers Work: Hands On!," January 5, 2018, YouTube, https://www.youtube.com/watch?v=Ct0wFde9XcI.

3 Joshua Davis, "Steeples," posted October 4, 2018, for Paint A Cell Tower Challenge, host James Gurney, September 30, 2018, Facebook, https://www.facebook.com/photo.php?fbid=10214338324544232&set=pcb.177115893179370&type=3&theater.

4 Telephone interview with Pastor Richard Colhouer, New Life Tabernacle Church, Tampa, Florida, January 10, 2019.

5 Ibid.

6 "Huge Cell Tower Disguised as a Cross," May 30, 2017, YouTube, https://www.youtube.com/watch?v=IWlB0s5_M2s.

7 Arthur C. Clarke, *Profiles of the Future: An Inquiry Into the Limits of the Possible* (New York: Harper & Row, 1973), 21 (note 1).

8 Peter Bebergal, *Strange Frequencies: The Extraordinary Story of the Technological Quest for the Supernatural* (New York: Tarcherperigee/Random House, 2018), 181-2.

9 Anthony Dunne, *Hertzian Tales: Electronic Products, Aesthetic Experience, and Critical Design* (Cambridge, Massachusetts, and London: MIT Press, 2018), 101.

10 Ibid., 102.

11 A mocking modifier in today's jargon for any belief in "out-there" supernatural forces, "woo-woo," may be an imitation of the sounds made by theremins and Moog synthesizers on science-fiction and horror movie soundtracks. On the Moog's eerie sounds and movie soundtracks, see Kristen Gallerneaux, *High Static, Dead Lines: Sonic Spectres and the Object Hereafter* (London: Strange Attractor Press/MIT Press, 2018), 213-21 (217).

12 Anthony Dunne, *Hertzian Tales: Electronic Products, Aesthetic Experience, and Critical Design* (Cambridge, Massachusetts, and London: MIT Press, 2018), 102.

13 On EVP and the ethereal haunting of sound technologies (including telephone and radio), see Kristen Gallerneaux, *High Static, Dead Lines*, 10-11.

14 Peter Bebergall, *Strange Frequencies*, 119-20.

15 Stephen King, *Cell: A Novel* (New York: Simon & Schuster, 2016).

16 Ibid., 450, 184.

17 Ibid., 111.

18 Ibid., 131.

19 Kristen Gallerneaux, *High Static, Dead Lines,* 13.

20 Ibid., 81.

21 Ibid., 81–3. Gallerneaux links Squier's "tree telephony" to his invention of Muzak, and notes the subsequent rise of digital streaming audio.

Chapter 5

1 Vincze Miklós, "These Beautiful Giant Sculptures Support Power Lines With Style," *Gizmodo*, io9, September 4, 2014, https://io9.gizmodo.com/these-beautiful-giant-sculptures-support-power-lines-wi-1630435303.

2 Donald Norman, *Emotional Design: Why We Love (or Hate) Everyday Things* (New York: Basic Books, 2005), Kindle ed., loc. 51.

3 Ibid., loc. 670.

4 Mark Favermann, "The Unaesthetic American Cell Tower: Ma Bell's Children Are Philistines," Berkshire Fine Arts,

November 25, 2012, http://www.berkshirefinearts.com/11-25-2012_the-unaesthetic-american-cell-tower.htm.

5   "Call Angel," Favermann Design website, http://www.favermanndesign.com/pages/call_angel.shtml.

6   Calzavara website, https://calzavara.it/about-us/.

7   Ibid., https://calzavara.it/cell-towers-urban-furniture/cell-tower-design-mosaictower/.

8   Allison C. Meier, "The Talking Statues of Rome," *JSTOR Daily*, June 18, 2018, https://daily.jstor.org/the-talking-statues-of-rome/.

9   Parson Animals, Videosystems website, https://videosystems.it/en/parson/parson-animals/.

10   Calzavara website, https://www.dicecell.it/#/1.

11   Skylar Tibbits, "The Emergence of '4D Printing,'" TED, February 2013, https://www.ted.com/talks/skylar_tibbits_the_emergence_of_4d_printing?language=en.

12   Skylar Tibbits, "To Bring Things to Life," BSH Home Appliances Group, June 29, 2017, YouTube, https://www.youtube.com/watch?time_continue=225&v=MxCfB-ar7M4.

13   "Look Again: Six Designers Take on Some of the World's Toughest Redesign Challenges," Introduction, Paola Antonelli; copy, Jon Gertner; illustration, Justin Metz, *The New York Times Magazine,* November 10, 2018, https://www.nytimes.com/interactive/2016/11/13/magazine/design-issue-redesign-challenge.html.

14   Skylar Tibbits, Alaska Design Forum, "360 North," April 6, 2018, YouTube, https://www.youtube.com/watch?time_continue=1886&v=hVFDjm0yvGc.

15   Antonio Sant'Elia, *Manifesto of Futurist Architecture*: https://www.abc.net.au/cm/lb/4285602/data/manifesto-of-futurist-architecture-data.pdf.

16 John K. Waters, *Blobitecture: Waveform Architecture and Digital Design* (Beverly, Massachusetts: Rockport Publishers, 2003).

17 President Donald J. Trump on Twitter, February 21, 2019, demonstrated the kind of vague boosterism that often characterizes discussions about 5G: "I want 5G, and even 6G, technology in the United States as soon as possible. It is far more powerful, faster, and smarter than the current standard. American companies must step up their efforts, or get left behind." The term itself is widely misunderstood. AT&T's current "5G Evolution," for example, is really just a branding effort for a "improved" 4G LTE.

Chapter 6

1 Nickolay Lamm, "What If [You] Could See Your Cellular Network?" December 21, 2013, August 26, 2018; accessed via Internet Archive, June 2019, https://web.archive.org/web/20 180826065319/http://nickolaylamm.com/art-for-clients/wh at-if-could-see-your-cellular-network/.

2 Liz Phair, "Stratford-On-Guy," *Exile in Guyville*, Matador Records, 1993.

3 Guowang Miao et al., *Fundamentals of Mobile Data Networks* (Cambridge: Cambridge University Press, 2016), 7 (Fig. 1.2), https://doi.org/10.1017/CBO9781316534298. Shannon Mattern sums it up: "Network architects have to negotiate between the idealized 'cell' architecture, the not-so-geometrically uniform, urban terrain, and the potentially variable user demand," in *Code and Clay, Data and Dirt; Five Thousand Years of Urban Media* (Minneapolis: University of Minnesota Press, 2017), 34.

4 Brian Hayes, *Infrastructure: A Field Guide to the Industrial Landscape* (New York and London, W. W. Norton & Co., 2005), 306.

5 Tas Anjarwalla, "Inventor of Cell Phone: We Knew Someday Everybody Would Have One," CNN, n.d., http://www.cnn.com/2010/TECH/mobile/07/09/cooper.cell.phone.inventor/index.html?hpt=Sbin.

6 An exception is Ted Oehmke, "Cell Phones Ruin the Opera? Meet the Culprit," *The New York Times*, January 6, 2000, https://www.nytimes.com/2000/01/06/technology/cell-phones-ruin-the-opera-meet-the-culprit.html.

7 Motorola news release, April 3, 1973, https://www.motorola.com/sites/default/files/library/us/about-motorola-history-milestones/pdfs/DynaTAC_newsrelease_73_001.pdf.

8 "Advanced Mobile Phone Service (AMPS)," AT&T film, 1978, YouTube, https://www.youtube.com/watch?v=d6X_1PcR_gs.

9 Motorola news release, April 3, 1973, https://www.motorola.com/sites/default/files/library/us/about-motorola-history-milestones/pdfs/DynaTAC_newsrelease_73_001.pdf.

10 American Futures, "The Town Where High Tech Meets a 1950s Lifestyle," *The Atlantic,* December 8, 2014, https://www.theatlantic.com/video/index/383477/the-west-virginia-town-that-banned-cell-phones/; Eun Kyung Kim, "This Town Lives Without Cell Phones, WiFi: Meet Green Bank, West Virginia," NBC *Today*, January 29, 2016, https://www.today.com/health/town-lives-without-cell-phones-wi-fi-meet-green-bank-t69911; "The US Town With No Cell Phones or Wi-Fi," *National Geographic* video, October 10, 2014, https://video.nationalgeographic.com/video/news/00000148-cd25-d00e-adef-cfb5ff9e0000.

11   Michael J. Gaynor, "The Town Without Wi-Fi," *Washingtonian,* January 4, 2015, https://www.washingtonian.com/2015/01/04/the-town-without-wi-fi/.

12   Ibid.

13   Kashmir Hill, "There's Wi-Fi in the Middle of the Only Place in the US Where Wi-Fi Is 'Outlawed,'" *Splinter*, December 22, 2015, https://splinternews.com/theres-wi-fi-in-the-middle-of-the-only-place-in-the-u-s-1793853672.

14   "Sugar Grove Naval Station," *e-WV: The West Virginia Encyclopedia,* December 12, 2016, https://www.wvencyclopedia.org/articles/2421.

15   *The Wire*, Season 3; see especially Episode 11.

16   Jessica Anderson, "Sun Investigates: Cellphone Surveillance Seen Years Earlier in 'The Wire,'" *The Baltimore Sun,* April 11, 2015, https://www.baltimoresun.com/news/maryland/investigations/bs-md-sun-investigates-stingray-20150410-story.html.

17   Justin Fenton and Justin George, "Conviction Vacated, New Trial Granted for Adnan Syed of 'Serial,'" *The Baltimore Sun,* June 30, 2016, https://www.baltimoresun.com/news/maryland/crime/bs-md-ci-adnan-syed-new-trial-201606 30-story.html.

18   HBO special, *The Case Against Adnan Syed*, broadcast spring 2019.

19   *Undisclosed* podcast, https://undisclosed-podcast.com/episodes/season-1/; AT&T cover sheet, *Undisclosed* podcast, https://undisclosed-podcast.com/docs/8/Fax%20Cover%20from%20ATT.pdf.

20   Douglas Starr, "What Your Cell Phone Can't Tell the Police," *The New Yorker,* June 26, 2014, https://www.newyorker.com/news/news-desk/what-your-cell-phone-cant-tell-the-police.

21 HBO special, *The Case Against Adnan Syed,* Part 2, broadcast spring 2019.

22 Ariana Kelly writes about the phone booth as a haunting transitional object in *Phone Booth* (New York and London: Bloomsbury Academic, 2015).

23 Jennifer Valentino-DeVries, "Tracking Phones, Google is a Dragnet for Police," *The New York Times,* April 13, 2019, https://nyti.ms/2UzEhUM.

24 Jessica Conditt, "'To Live and Die in LA' Shows How Much Google Knows About You," *Engadget*, May 15, 2019, https://www.engadget.com/2019/05/15/google-privacy-serial-live-die-la-true-crime-podcast/.

25 "Doug Aitken's *New Era*," *The New York Times*, video, April 5, 2018, https://www.nytimes.com/video/t-magazine/100000005833662/doug-aitkens-new-era.html.

Chapter 7

1 Udit Narayana Kar and Debarshi Kumar Sanyal, "An overview of device-to-device communication in cellular networks," *ICT Express* 4.4 (December 2018), 203–8, https://doi.org/10.1016/j.icte.2017.08.002.

2 Michel Serres, *Hominescence,* trans. Randolph Burks (London and New York: Bloomsbury Academic, 2019; originally published 2001), 139.

3 Ibid., 140.

4 Ibid., 141.

5 Serres argues that "the portable cell phone and laptop have liberated addresses from places . . . Absent from the local, we find ourselves present in global space" (ibid., 180), a formulation that sounds a lot like 1990s rhetoric about cyberspace as a stateless and lawless transcendental realm.

6   Timothy Morton, *Hyperobjects: Philosophy and Ecology after the End of the World* (Minneapolis: University of Minnesota Press, 2013), Kindle ed., loc. 104.

7   Ibid., loc. 127.

8   Ibid., loc. 453.

9   US Fish and Wildlife Service website, "Communication Towers," https://www.fws.gov/birds/bird-enthusiasts/threats -to-birds/collisions/communication-towers.php.

10   Sarah Knapton, "Electromagnetic Radiation from Power Lines and Phone Masts Poses 'Credible' Threat to Wildlife, Report Finds," *The Telegraph,* May 18, 2018, https://www.telegraph.co. uk/science/2018/05/17/electromagnetic-radiation-power-l ines-phone-masts-poses-credible/; Douglas Quenqua, "Radio Signals Skew Birds' Internal Navigation," *The New York Times,* May 12, 2014, https://www.nytimes.com/2014/05/13/science/ radio-signals-skew-birds-internal-navigation.html.

11   Dan Garisto, "Birds Get Their Internal Compass from this Newly ID'd Eye Protein," *Science News*, April 3, 2018, https:// www.sciencenews.org/article/birds-get-their-internal- compass-newly-id-eye-protein; Roswitha Wiltschko and Wolfgang Wiltschko, "Sensing Magnetic Directions in Birds: Radical Pair Processes Involving Cryptochrome," *Biosensors* 4.3 (September 2014), 221–42. Morton understands this phenomenon in terms of quantum physics, suggesting that "a bird detects the quantum signature of an electromagnetic wave, not the wave itself," *Hyperobjects: Philosophy and Ecology after the End of the World* (Minneapolis: University of Minnesota Press, 2013), Kindle ed., loc. 856.

12 Osprey Watch website, http://www.osprey-watch.org/learn-about-osprey/build-an-osprey-nest/.

13 Jordan Teicher, "The Abandoned Microwave Towers that Once Linked the US," *Wired,* March 10, 2015, https://www.wired.com/2015/03/spencer-harding-the-long-lines/.

14 Spencer James Harding, The Long Lines website (for a photo book), http://spencerjharding.com/project/the-long-lines/.

15 Photos of the site on file suggest it was constructed between March 1975 and February 1976. My thanks to Terry Hinton and Jim Gale of the Monroe County, Florida Property Appraisals Office.

16 Monroe County construction permit no. 00086740000100, October 12, 2012.

17 "Florida's Forgotten Tourist Tower," *Crow's Nest,* February 2, 2015, http://crowsneststpete.com/2015/02/02/floridas-forgotten-tourist-tower/.

18 Ibid.

19 Thomas Neil Knowles, "The US Navy Wireless Telegraph Stations at Key West and Dry Tortugas," *Florida Keys Sea Heritage Journal* 19.1 (Fall 2008), 1–16. The following paragraphs about Key West and its towers are based on Knowles' article and photo-illustrations.

20 Walter Benjamin, *The Arcades Project,* trans. Howard Eiland and Kevin McLaughlin (Cambridge, Massachusetts, and London: Belknap Press of Harvard University Press, 1999), 887.

21 Ibid., 459, quoting Sigfried Giedion, *Bauen in Frankreich Eisen Eisonbeton* (Leipzig and Berlin: Klinkhardt & Biermann, 1928), 7.

22   Devin Coldewey, "Ubiquitilink Advance Means Every Phone Is Now a Satellite Phone," *Techcrunch,* February 25, 2019, https://techcrunch.com/2019/02/25/ubiquitilink-advance-means-every-phone-is-now-a-satellite-phone/.

23   UbiquityLink website, https://lynk.world. (The company changed its name to Lynk in autumn 2019.)

24   Ibid.

25   Tracy Samuelson, "After Sandy, Questions Linger Over Cellphone Reliability," "All Tech Considered," *Morning Edition*, National Public Radio, April 29, 2013, https://www.npr.org/sections/alltechconsidered/2013/04/29/179243218/after-sandy-questions-linger-over-cellphone-reliability.

INDEX

Note: Page numbers followed by "f" indicate figures.